Haunted Girl

ESTHER COX & THE GREAT AMHERST MYSTERY

LAURIE GLENN NORRIS WITH BARBARA THOMPSON

Copyright © 2012, Laurie Glenn Norris and Barbara Thompson

All rights reserved. No part of this book may be reproduced, stored in a retrieval system or transmitted in any form or by any means without the prior written permission from the publisher, or, in the case of photocopying or other reprographic copying, permission from Access Copyright, 1 Yonge Street, Suite 1900, Toronto, Ontario M5E 1E5.

Nimbus Publishing Limited
3731 Mackintosh St, Halifax, NS B3K 5A5
(902) 455-4286 nimbus.ca

Printed and bound in Canada

Author photo: LGN: Harvey's Foto Source, Fredericton, NB
Design: Margaret Issenman

Library and Archives Canada Cataloguing in Publication
    Glenn Norris, Laurie, 1957-
    Haunted girl : Esther Cox & the great Amherst mystery / Laurie Glenn Norris with Barbara Thompson.
    Also issued in electronic format.
    ISBN 978-1-55109-907-1

1. Cox, Esther, 1860-1912. 2. Ghosts—Nova Scotia—Amherst. 3. Haunted houses—Nova Scotia—Amherst. 4. Amherst (N.S.)—Biography. I. Thompson, Barbara II. Title.
BF1027.C69G64 2012   130.92   C2011-907631-4

Nimbus Publishing acknowledges the financial support for its publishing activities from the Government of Canada through the Canada Book Fund (CBF) and the Canada Council for the Arts, and from the Province of Nova Scotia through the Department of Communities, Culture and Heritage.

Contents

Preface ⊰ 1 ⊱

Chapter 1: Setting the Stage ⊰ 3 ⊱
Chapter 2: The Great Amherst Mystery Unfolds ⊰ 22 ⊱
Chapter 3: Cashing In on the Great Amherst Mystery ⊰ 35 ⊱
Chapter 4: Living Among Spirits ⊰ 59 ⊱
Chapter 5: Life Afterwards ⊰ 76 ⊱
Chapter 6: What They Thought It Was ⊰ 100 ⊱
Chapter 7: A Haunted Girl ⊰ 121 ⊱
Chapter 8: The Legacy of the Great Amherst Mystery ⊰ 151 ⊱

⊱

Acknowledgements ⊰ 158 ⊱
Selected Bibliography ⊰ 161 ⊱
Photo Credits ⊰ 165 ⊱
Index ⊰ 166 ⊱

Dedicated to my parents, Annie and Reg Glenn

For Esther

Preface

*Strange things may be generally accounted
for if their cause is fairly searched out.*
~ Jane Austen

The series of events that became known as the Great Amherst Mystery occurred between 1878 and 1879 in Amherst, Nova Scotia. At the centre of these events was Esther Cox, an eighteen-year-old girl from a working-class family. For a year and three months, Esther allegedly was haunted by ghostly spirits that rapped on walls and floors, set fire to clothes, curtains, and woodwork, moved furniture and other household objects, wrote scurrilous messages, stabbed, scratched, and pinched her, and threatened to take her life.

Crowds gathered in and around the Princess Street house where Esther lived with her family to witness what were known as "the manifestations." Esther became a local celebrity, with newspaper reporters following her every move and prominent citizens observing and testing her—was she a medium, magnet, or battery?—in hopes of solving the Mystery. Some observers perceived Esther's experiences as the work of the devil, some saw them as the effects of electricity or mesmerism, still others were certain they were of Esther's own manufacture. She was regarded as both a victim and a trickster.

Esther's own voice and thoughts, unfortunately, are lost forever to us, overshadowed by the actions and words of the doctors, clergy, newspapermen, and opportunists whose opinions counted for more than hers. And she left behind no known diaries, letters, or writings that might have provided valuable insight into her state of mind during this extraordinary period.

How the Great Amherst Mystery is regarded by those who grew up hearing the story or who created the books, plays, and Internet entries about it has been influenced by the subjective writings of a single individual determined to use Esther's plight for his own gain. But his is only one side of the story. There is much more to tell.

CHAPTER 1

Setting the Stage

This town has its mystery at last. Occurrences strange to all who have witnessed them have for several nights transpired at the house of a responsible and reliable citizen.
~ *Chignecto Post*, September 19, 1878

The Great Amherst Mystery began with a cardboard box that would not behave itself. On September 9, 1878, eighteen-year-old Esther Cox and her sister Jennie had just settled down for the night when they heard a strange noise coming from beneath their bed. They knew that the only thing under there was a box full of old fabric patches. The girls hung over the edge of the bed and peeked, upside down, at the box. It was moving back and forth. After agreeing that the noise was likely from a mouse making its nest for the night, Esther and Jennie thought no more about it, and soon both of them were fast asleep.

The following night, the box became even more active. This time it moved out from under the bed to the middle of the room. Esther and Jennie watched as it threw off its cover and turned over on one side, spilling patches out onto the floor. One brave girl got up, replaced the fabric and the cover, and scurried back to bed. The pesky box once again moved about and dumped its contents. By this time, Esther and Jennie had become truly alarmed, and called for their brother, William Cox, and brother-in-law, John Teed, to come into the room to witness what was happening. The young men initially laughed and dismissed the idea of a box of fabric moving about on its own, but the girls asked them to stay for a few minutes longer and see what might happen next. William and John sat at the edge of the bed waiting, but the box remained still. Then someone suggested that the lamp on the bureau be turned down. This was done, and, to the astonishment of the witnesses, almost immediately the box's cover flew off and the container turned over on its side. Jennie promptly fainted.

The next night, it was the girls' bed that suddenly came to life. Esther and Jennie could feel their quilt and blanket slowly moving, being pulled downward to the bottom of the bed by an unseen force. They called William and John to witness what was going on. The bedclothes were replaced and, with the lamp turned low, the four waited to see what would happen. This time the covers crept slowly, by degrees, toward Esther's side of the bed. The pillows began to move that way as well, only more quickly. John jumped up and grabbed one of them. He felt a jerking motion, and when he let go, the pillow flew to the bottom of the bed.

The two girls were greatly upset by these nightly happenings, but things were about to get a lot worse. The next evening, soon after she and Jennie had retired, Esther leapt from the bed screaming that she was dying. Jennie quickly lit the lamp and was shocked to see her sister standing in the middle of the room holding tightly to the back of a chair, her nails digging into the wood. Esther's hair was standing on end, her face was red, and her eyes were bulging out of their sockets. Jennie called for help. John and William rushed into the room, this time followed by Olive Teed, the girls' older sister, and Daniel, her husband. Esther was assisted back to bed, where she sat for a moment. She then jumped to her feet once more and screamed that she was going to burst into pieces. As her family looked on, Esther's body swelled and she alternately screamed and ground her teeth. These convulsions lasted until a loud noise, like a clap of thunder, boomed through the room. A moment later, three more reports, that seemed to come from under the bed, shook the whole house. Esther's swelling began to subside. In a few minutes it was gone, and she slept peacefully through the rest of the night.

Each evening, after this frightening first episode, Esther continued to experience painful swelling, accompanied by the twitching of her arms and legs. Sometimes she appeared to be in a trance. Her physical suffering seemed to be relieved only when the thunderous noises began, either as rapping sounds emanating from under the bed or as knocking sounds on the roof of the house. These loud nightly noises began to attract the attention of neighbours, who were curious to know what was going on.

Olive and Daniel, at their wits' end, summoned Dr. Thomas Carritte, the family physician, to have a look at Esther and see what he could make of her condition. On his first evening at her bedside, Dr. Carritte witnessed the swelling and other symptoms and treated her for what he called "nervous prostration." He administered the standard medication for rattled nerves: powdered laudanum mixed with water and alcohol to relieve any pain and calm Esther's irritation.

Dr. Carritte's ministrations did not help much. Almost nightly, throughout the rest of September and into October,

Esther and Jennie's bedroom was a scene of turmoil. The quilts and sheets continued to move off the bed and the pillows took on a life of their own, swelling and deflating and moving about the room. While Esther continued to grow feverish and her body ballooned and trembled, other more disturbing symptoms emerged. Esther, while in a trance, often went through the motions of having sexual intercourse.

Until the unsettling events of the Great Amherst Mystery began, Esther Cox's life had been much like that of any other young woman living in the mid-nineteenth-century Maritime provinces. The youngest child of Archibald Thompson Cox and Esther Logan Fisher, she was born on March 28, 1860, in Eastville, Colchester County, Nova Scotia, a tiny community located near the head of the Stewiacke Valley, one of the province's most fertile farming regions. Fringed by the Cobequid Mountains, the valley spans western Pictou County and into Colchester County as far as the Shubenacadie River. In Colchester County, the valley is divided into three sections known as Upper, Middle, and Lower Stewiacke. Eastville and other small communities grew up on either side of the Stewiacke River, which runs the entire length of the valley. In addition to its family farms, by the 1870s Eastville also contained a church, schoolhouse, hotel, two blacksmith shops, and a sawmill.

Esther and her siblings were fifth-generation Irish. The Cox family, of United Empire Loyalist stock, had lived in New Hampshire before moving to Nova Scotia in the 1700s. Esther's father, Archibald, son of William and Olive Jane Cox, was born in the 1820s and was only a year old when his father died of

Archibald T. Cox Jr., Esther's stepbrother.

smallpox. Shortly after, Olive Jane married Eleazar Boyd Dickey and went on to have more children.

Archibald and Esther Cox had six children, starting with Olive, born in 1850, William, Abigail (who died as a toddler), Nellie, Jennie, and Esther, all born two years apart. Esther's mother died when her namesake was a mere three weeks old. The child spent her early life in the care of her paternal grandmother, Olive Jane, and step-grandfather, Eleazar Dickey. Archibald, with other children to care for, would have had little choice but to hand the infant over to someone who could care for her properly. According to family legend, Esther was a tiny baby; at the age of nine months she still weighed only five pounds.

Archibald did not remain a widower for long. When Esther was two years old, he married Mary Cox of Stewiacke, who may have been a distant relative. But he soon found himself a widower once again when Mary died due to complications from childbirth. By July 1866 Archibald had left Eastville and was living in Halifax, working as a porter and married, for the third time, to Ann McIntosh. Archibald and Ann went on to have two sons, half-brothers to Esther and her siblings. A few years later, Archibald, Ann, and this new family moved from Halifax to Machias, Maine, where Archibald was employed in the lumbering industry.

By the time Esther was six years old, she and her siblings had experienced considerable turmoil in their lives. Their own mother dead, they had had two step-mothers and had become separated from both their father, who was far away, and from each other, living with different families in the Stewiacke area.

The Dickeys ran a farm, and Grandmother Dickey was in charge of the post office, located in a room of the house. Her responsibilities as postmistress meant that their home was a community centre, a place where people would meet to mail and pick up letters and parcels and to exchange news about the community and beyond.

As a young child, Esther tagged along as her grandmother fed the chickens and gathered eggs, and she played with her older siblings who lived close by. Jennie and Nellie, two and four years older, may have been in charge of looking after their baby sister while Grandmother Dickey weeded the garden or milked the cows. As she grew older, Esther assisted her grandmother with cooking and baking and the making of jams, pickles, and other preserves. She was also responsible for the weekly chore of washing the family's clothes.

Along with their strong work ethic, the Cox and Dickey families, like the rest of the Stewiacke Valley residents, were deeply religious members of an active Christian community

Springside United Church in Eastville, NS. Esther attended this church with her grandmother Olive Dickey.

and attended church regularly. The Dickeys were members of the Presbyterian Springside Church in Eastville. Presbyterian ministers, along with the governing body known as Elders, were an influential and dominant presence in the community. The Elders, all men, were respected, and sometimes feared, by their congregation. The community turned to them for advice, and all were conscious of conducting themselves, in all aspects of their lives, in a manner respectful to and approved of by the church. The Elders, while insisting upon strict adherence to Presbyterian doctrine, also espoused the importance of hard work and a well-rounded education.

Going to church was not only a duty; it was also a social activity—a weekly opportunity to chat with neighbours and friends and catch up on the news. In the summertime, prayer meetings—all-day events consisting of sermons, meals, and prayers—were held outdoors, along the river or in a field or forest clearing. During the colder months, everyone moved inside the church or to private homes for prayer sessions and fundraising events.

Church attendance was not the only form of socializing in the Eastville area. Barn, house, or mill raisings, called frolics, were also popular community gatherings. The women prepared copious amounts of food, setting up tables in the yard or on the grass while the men and boys were busy with their construction projects. Frolics usually ended with an evening dance. Farmer James Johnson from Burnside, a community near Eastville, recorded in his diary that on October 4, 1868, he attended a house frolic at the home of his brother Sam and that on December 30th, he "went to a candy spree at John Deyarmond's." Grandmother Dickey, with eight-year-old Esther in tow, may well have attended these events.

Women also gathered for quilting bees and mat-hooking sessions. Like the frolics, these community activities served as a social outlet while accomplishing necessary and practical tasks. Quilts and mats were needed to keep the family warm and comfortable in the winter, and also were a requirement for every girl's hope chest. Young adults, for their part, socialized and got a break from the tedious winter weather and watchful parents by going on straw rides. Piling into a straw-filled bobsled and covering themselves with robes and blankets, the youngsters—and their chaperones—would drive out into the evening, perhaps to a local lumber camp or someone's home for refreshments and singing. For those with a taste for cultural pastimes, there were amateur dramatics societies, and music and literary clubs.

Obtaining a formal education also played a role in the lives of Stewiacke Valley residents. The lane leading up to the

Eastville School, which Esther attended. Today it is the Eastville Hall.

one-room Eastville schoolhouse was across the main road from the Dickey farm, so distance would not have been a deterrent to Esther's schooling. She shared a desk with another little girl and printed, drew, and wrote her lessons on a slate with a piece of chalk. At recess the children played hide-and-seek in the schoolyard and in the rolling green fields behind the building. As an adult, Esther was able to read and write, but how proficiently and with what level of formal education is not known. School attendance was likely intermittent at best for Esther, her siblings, and friends; children were needed at home to help with the chores, and schooling was limited to six months of the year.

For most families in a community like Eastville, knowing how to read and do sums were the skills considered most useful to manage a farm and a household. Presbyterians, however, placed a high value on education as a means of creating a more useful and productive earthly life. Eastville's schoolteacher would have taught grammar, history, literature, and poetry, along with the basics, and would have led the students in art, music, and drawing if she had had the skill and inclination to do so. Any further education would have been beyond the financial resources and practical needs of most of the valley's families.

In July 1874, when Esther was fourteen, her eldest sister, Olive—then twenty-four and living in Amherst, Nova Scotia, having been lured there in the hope of securing a husband and, second best, of finding work as a maid, cleaning woman, or seamstress—married Daniel Teed. Sometime after that, the rest of the Cox siblings moved from Eastville to Amherst in search of a livelihood beyond that which farm life could offer. Coming from a rural area, Esther would have found this bustling town a much more exciting place to live than Eastville. It certainly presented her with greater possibilities for both work and romance.

Esther would have been aware of how important it was for a young woman to secure a beau and, ultimately, a husband. She and her sisters likely discussed their future husbands and lives in detail.

In 1878, when the events of the Mystery began, Esther Cox was a short, plump eighteen-year-old with curly, shoulder-length, dark brown hair, large grey-blue eyes, and a fair complexion. She, like most young women of her time, had been brought up to act like a lady whose conduct was above reproach. Grandmother Dickey would have taught Esther to respect her elders, be quiet and modest, and do nothing to draw attention to her person or actions. Her life was expected to revolve around the home, with her wants and needs subservient to those of the male members of the family. Such expectations, backed up by the church, the community, and common practice, meant that she was to live a retiring life, away from the public eye. And until the strange events of the Great Amherst Mystery, Esther seems to have adhered to this code of conduct.

From a young age, however, Esther also showed signs of rebellion. She liked to get her own way, and was often stubborn and moody until she did. Family members walked on eggshells when Esther was not pleased about something, and there was no peace in the house until she was satisfied.

Some time after their wedding, Daniel and Olive Teed moved into spacious rental accommodations at 6 Princess Street, Amherst. The room was needed, for by September 1878, two children, William and George, had been added to the young family. Also living with them were Daniel's brother John, Olive's brother William, and sisters Jennie (considered the family beauty), Nellie, and Esther. As a child, Esther may well have been doted upon by her grandparents and the centre of attention in their home, but in Daniel's crowded house the two little boys stole the spotlight. And brother-in-law Daniel, if not legally responsible for her, as head of the household was accountable for her conduct and that of all the inhabitants of 6 Princess Street. Esther and the other family members were expected to follow Olive's lead and obey him. Daniel's authority, however, was soon to be challenged.

Daniel Teed was born in 1848 in Malagash, a tiny farming and fishing community on the peninsula of the same name in northwest Cumberland County, Nova Scotia. His ancestors were the first English-speaking settlers in the area: six Teed brothers, United Empire Loyalists all, moved there after the American Revolution. One of their descendants, John Teed, and his wife, Martha Ralph, had ten children, of whom Daniel was the eldest. John was a shoemaker, and Daniel followed his father into that occupation.

Daniel, an honest man, was liked and respected by all who knew him, as was Olive, a hard-working homemaker. The inhabitants of the Teed household were regular churchgoers who read the Bible, prayed, and sang hymns in their home. The Teeds were Methodists and maintained a family pew at the Trinity Methodist Church. Daniel was also a member of a local temperance society. The pastor of Trinity Methodist was the popular Reverend Robert Alder Temple, noted as both a champion of the temperance movement and an eloquent speaker. Esther sometimes attended Trinity Methodist Church with Daniel, Olive, and their sons, but more often she went to Christ Church, the local Anglican house of worship, with sister Jennie.

In 1878, Amherst was a small town of about 3,500 people. It was also the economic and social centre of Cumberland County and, as one of the fastest-growing industrial communities in

View of Amherst, NS, from *Canadian Illustrated News*, December 9, 1876, by Albert J. Hill.

the Maritimes, it was a boomtown, soon to be known as "Busy Amherst." Horses and wagons moved up and down its dirt-filled streets while its wooden sidewalks were alive with people going to and from work, shopping, and making social calls. Amherst's flourishing economy drew people from around the county, the province, and beyond to work in its factories and foundries and the spin-off jobs they created. The town's largest employers included A. Robb and Sons, where the first telephone in the Maritimes was installed in 1877, Rhodes and Curry Co., Christie Brothers, and the Amherst Foundry, all started and managed by ambitious, hard-working men out to make their fortunes.

    The Teed house was in the heart of downtown Amherst, surrounded by a mix of businesses, rented workers' houses, and homes of prominent citizens. The Holmes Carriage Factory, which included a blacksmith shop, was nearby. Blair's Stables was a mere four hundred feet away, while opposite was the large garden of Reverend Nathan Tupper, co-founder of the local drug store and brother of Father of Confederation and future prime minister Sir Charles Tupper.

The Teeds' rented house was relatively new, having been built by owner James Fillmore in 1859. It was a two-storey dwelling, painted yellow, with a yard extending around the house to a barn at the back. The first floor contained six rooms: a parlour, dining room, kitchen, pantry, sewing room, and hallway. Olive grew geraniums in the parlour's large bay windows. The pantry, where the family kept its dishes, cookware, and baking and food supplies, was located off the kitchen. The front hall had a stairway that led to the second floor. The four small upstairs bedrooms, each with a window and door, were entered separately from a hallway. There was no entryway between the bedrooms. Two faced onto Princess Street, while the other two, at the back of the house, overlooked the barn. The house had an attic as well as a cellar where the family stored potatoes, root vegetables, and coal.

While Esther stayed at home to help Olive look after the children and do the housework, Jennie was employed as a seamstress by James Dunlap, a local businessman. Daniel, John, and William all worked for the Amherst Boot and Shoe Company, another major employer in the town, which made footwear for men, women, and children, and also produced and repaired horse harnesses and collars and other leather tack in its harness shop. Its offices and factory were located near the corner of Church and Victoria streets, just a ten-minute walk from Princess Street. A relatively new business, Amherst Boot and Shoe had been incorporated in 1867, and its roster of directors and investors included some of the most influential names in

Employees at Dunlap and Cook Co., where Jennie Cox worked as a seamstress.

Cumberland County society, including three of the four Fathers of Confederation born in the county: R. B. Dickey, Jonathan McCully, and Sir Charles Tupper.

Besides the Teeds, another of Amherst Boot and Shoe's many employees was a distant cousin of Daniel's, Bob MacNeill. He was also Esther's beau. Bob, a good-looking young man of twenty-three with dark eyes, black hair, and moustache, looked the part of a romantic hero. Like Daniel, Bob was a native of Malagash and from another of the first families of the area. He was a descendent of Neill MacNeill, one of twelve Scottish brothers who immigrated to North America around 1800. Neill MacNeill had settled in Malagash, where he raised two families.

West Victoria Street, Amherst, circa 1895.

His first wife was Eleanor Teed. Their son Samuel married Susan Simpson and they, in turn, had ten children. Robert (Bob) Alder Temple MacNeill, the second-eldest son, was born on January 29, 1855. Interestingly, the MacNeills, who, like the Teeds, were Methodists, named Bob after the well-liked Reverend Temple. The Reverend was certainly a role model whom god-fearing parents of the time would wish their sons to emulate.

From the age of fourteen, Bob MacNeill had walked with the aid of a crutch. One day in the winter of 1869, the family's pigs escaped from their pen and he went running after them. Tripping over a frozen wheel rut, Bob dislocated his right kneecap. The local physician was called in and decided that, to reduce the swelling, the fluid on the knee should be drained. The doctor secured Bob's leg to the floor and bored a hole through his kneecap to let the fluid escape. What the doctor actually did was drain the water off the joint, and the leg stiffened. The injured knee developed a permanent bend, and Bob's right foot

Amherst Boot and Shoe, circa 1895.

could no longer touch the ground. A T-shaped crutch was made for him, and he quickly became proficient in its use.

In fact, Bob McNeill, using his crutch and one good leg, could run faster than most men. He could drive horses and, while sitting down, split wood. Over time, he developed great upper-body strength. Still, his parents worried about how he would earn a living. They certainly thought him unable to run the family farm, which instead would be willed to two of his four brothers. Since he was not an able-bodied man in the traditional sense, it was decided that he should pursue work he could perform while seated. So Bob moved to Amherst sometime in the 1870s to learn the trade of shoemaking.

By the summer of 1878, Bob MacNeill and Esther Cox had known each other for a while and were often in each other's company. They were connected through family, through

Amherst Boot and Shoe packing room staff, 1914.

Daniel's work, and through the Trinity Methodist Church, which Bob also regularly attended. He often visited the Teed household, for meals and other family gatherings, and he and Esther had begun courting. Another of the Cox girls also had a beau at this time. On August 20, 1878, Esther's sister Nellie married James Snowden, a tailor. The newlyweds went off to live with the groom's parents in Sackville, New Brunswick.

On Wednesday, August 28, eight days after Nellie's wedding, Esther and Bob went for an evening buggy ride. Most people got around Amherst by walking, and a stroll through the town, especially around Christie's Pond, with an attractive partner would have been a pleasant outing. With his limp and crutch, however, Bob would not have been at his best while walking beside a sweetheart whom he wanted to impress, so he rented a horse and two-seater buggy. This method of transportation meant the couple could be alone, away from the scrutiny of the Teed family and the town in general.

Bob drove along Victoria Street, a main artery through Amherst. Both ends of the street led out into the countryside and had secondary roads leading to the Tantramar Marsh. Bob and Esther drove west out onto the marsh following the setting sun. While the weather that evening had started out fine, clouds were gathering quickly and soon a light drizzle was falling. No one knows what happened between Bob and Esther that evening, but hours later in the pouring rain, when she arrived back at the Teeds' front door, Esther was upset and crying and her clothing was soaked through.

Bob did not show up for work at Amherst Boot and Shoe the next day. He had left Amherst forever. Something—a lover's quarrel, or worse—had occurred between Bob MacNeill and Esther Cox on the evening of August 28, 1878, something that sparked a local phenomenon, an international sensation, and a legend: the Great Amherst Mystery.

CHAPTER 2

The Great Amherst Mystery Unfolds

The scenes around Mr. Teed's house have been such as to surprise and perplex hundreds of intelligent men of all classes who have gathered at the house night after night to hear, see and be thoroughly convinced that, whatever it may be, there is no fraud or deception on the parts of the inmates of the house.

The rappings which we have mentioned are of two kinds light and heavy or one may be termed a rapping and the other a pounding. It is the latter which is the most remarkable and which naturally fills the ordinary hearer with awe, it is liable to come at any time, but is always in Esther's vicinity.

~ *Colchester Sun*, November 6, 1878

It did not take long for the events at 6 Princess Street to attract the attention of the local press. Dr. Thomas Carritte, Esther's attending physician, told the *Chignecto Post*: "My attention was first called to taps apparently on the wooden slats of the bed, and I heard the straw in the straw tick rustle

6 Princess Street, Amherst, date unknown.

the same as if stirred by the hand when making the bed. Then the taps left the slats and commenced on the walls, like beating a tattoo. From the walls it ran to the roof, sounding like a heavy hammering. I heard these sounds repeatedly after my first visit. Sometimes other persons were present and heard the same." During one session of particularly loud pounding on the roof, the good doctor went outside to investigate. He recalled, it "seemed as if some person was on the roof with a heavy sledge hammer pounding away to try and break through the shingles."

These rapping and pounding noises could be heard both day and night and always in Esther's presence. At night they were concentrated in her bedroom and by day they occurred whenever she went to the barn to do her chores or down into the cellar. It sounded, said the *Post*, "as if a colossal fist were pounding on the beams with the fury of a demon. Other persons have accompanied her and have satisfied themselves that the noise was made by no human hand or by any agency visible to mortal eyes. It has a dead sound as if it were a flesh-covered fist." The rappings, the paper stated, were "to an unpractical ear suggestive of telegraphy, but it is not that, and is more like the tippy-ti tap of an idle and impatient boy."

The source of the rapping was also not without a sense of humour. According to the *Post*, "it is musical. It beats the measure of *Yankee Doodle* and *Someone's Tapping at the Garden Gate*, while it regularly keeps time with any tune which any one sings or whistles."

It also had a nasty side. Esther began to experience bodily attacks, not only at night but during the day as well. Frequently, loud slapping sounds could be heard throughout the house, and Esther would appear with conspicuous red marks on her cheeks. A number of visitors to the home claimed to have heard the sounds and seen Esther's injured face. Esther herself said that, on one occasion, she saw a large black hand reach out to strike her. And she was not its only victim. The *Post* reported that when three men went into the Teeds' cellar to investigate, "one of them received a violent blow on the forehead from this invisible Something."

It did not take long for Esther's plight to become known throughout the neighbourhood and beyond. The pounding on the roof of the house was audible from Blair's Stables, and people walking along Church Street could hear it clearly. On September 19, the *Post* claimed that "the affair has created great excitement, crowds having gathered about the house nightly, so that a policeman was required to disperse them."

While the number of curious bystanders who gathered outside the home was growing, Esther's bedroom was also getting crowded. Amherst's social elite beat a path to the Teeds' front door in parties reminiscent of those who gathered to view a hanging. A dozen or more at a time would surround Esther and Jennie as they lay in bed with the blankets agitating and the pillows leaping about. According to the *Post*, "two of her visitors tried to subdue her pillows but felt a weight of twenty-five or thirty pounds pulling against them. When it could not get away it elongated itself to its utmost capacity, just as a piece of elastic rubber would do, and wriggled and squirmed like a leach in a jar of water." Those who made it upstairs at 6 Princess Street, most often by Dr. Carritte's invitation, included entrepreneur James P. Dunlap, dentist Dr. E. D. McLean, shopkeeper William

Dr. Edwin Clay, minister and immigration agent who took an interest in the Great Amherst Mystery, travelled Nova Scotia and New Brunswick lecturing about it.

Sleep, and several ladies, all of whose respectability was beyond reproach.

The local clergy and physicians were also interested in what was happening. The Reverend Robert Temple came to observe the situation and offer his comfort and prayers. A number of his ministerial colleagues from other denominations came as well, including Reverend Ingram Sutcliff of Amherst and Dr. Edwin Clay, a Baptist minister from Pugwash, who claimed that he could put an end to the Mystery. After spending two days at the Teed home with Esther, however, he went away just as baffled as everyone else as to the cause of the manifestations. Dr. Nathan Tupper also visited, and was not in the least bit impressed with what he saw. While there were no occurrences in the bedroom during his visit, he told reporters that, if "a strong rawhide whip was laid across Esther's bare shoulders by a powerful arm the Mystery would be solved at once."

In a November 7 *Chignecto Post* article, we get an inkling of what Esther herself was thinking during this period. The story contained two long statements about the recent events surrounding the girl, one by Dr. Carritte and the other by Rev. Temple. We hear Esther's words filtered through those of Temple, who told reporters, "I can give no solution of this mystery. Miss Cox herself imagines she is under the influence of a young man, who appears to have picked up some books on mesmerism and becoming versed in it, has been experimenting on her. She is fully imbued with the idea that he controlled and influenced these movements." While Temple does not mention Bob MacNeill specifically, it is highly likely that the reverend was referring here to his namesake.

But Esther was not the only resident of 6 Princess Street to be tormented. One night, Esther and Jennie were lying in bed with Dr. Carritte in attendance when Jennie suddenly cried out, "Oh Doctor, it has got hold of me." After rushing to her side Carritte discovered that the front of Jennie's nightgown was torn open and her chest was covered with scratches. Not new ones, however—they appeared to be days old. Jennie told the doctor that "it" was pressing on her sides and painfully compressing her chest.

The noises and movement of inanimate objects continued to occur in the daytime as well as through the night. Chairs

Reverend Robert Alder Temple was the minister of the Amherst Methodist Church, which the Teed family attended. Bob MacNeill was his namesake.

followed Esther around. Once, she went into the pantry and closed the door, and when she attempted to step out into the kitchen again, she found all of Olive's wooden chairs piled up in front of the pantry door as if trying to follow her into the tiny room. Another time, while in the cellar, a basket of beets trailed along after her. Rev. Temple himself told the press that a pail of water would "be violently agitated into a whirlpool, and foam like the waves of the tides" whenever Esther came near it.

Esther also became an instrument for what was known as automatic writing. That is, she was overcome by a spirit or another supernatural force that guided her arm, and she was unable to stop its motion. She demonstrated this to onlookers by taking a pencil in her hand, standing before a wall in the house. Immediately, she would appear to lose control of her arm and hand, which would move of their own accord, causing Esther to create words and phrases she had no intention of producing. The *Post* reported that "some of these sentences are very wicked ones, and are most horribly profane."

Indeed, the best-known and most frequently described incident of the Mystery concerned this writing. One night, while Esther was in a trance-like state, and the family was assembled in the bedroom trying to comfort her and get her bedclothes to behave, a scratching sound was heard above the bed. Someone looked up and noticed words on the wall. On closer inspection with a lamp, the crudely scratched message was read aloud. "Esther Cox," it proclaimed, "you are mine to kill."

One evening in October 1878, J. Albert Black, editor of the *Chignecto Post*, visited the Teed home with Dr. Carritte. Black planned to contact and interview the source of the mysterious knocking which, by this time was recognized as some type of supernatural being and was referred to alternately, by the family and the press, as "the invisible rapper," "the force," and "the spirit." It was not obliging when Black first requested it to perform a number of feats. It warmed up, however, when the editor asked Esther to go to the cellar. As soon as she went downstairs, a series of rapid and heavy knocks was heard under the kitchen floor, below the feet of the newsman and doctor. As the sounds continued, they became louder and more forceful. The last of them shook the house. All at once they stopped and Esther cried out, "Oh, it's going to strike me!" She hastily ran back upstairs, telling Black and Carritte that "it" was in the habit of hitting her when the knocking stopped suddenly. Black later reported that Esther "seemed quite cheerful and said she had become so accustomed to the noises that she felt none of the fear she had experienced at first, and was only alarmed about being struck."

Next, Black, carrying a lamp and a pencil, accompanied Esther to the pantry. Esther held the pencil to the wall but her arm did not budge. When Black left the room, however, leaving Esther in the dark, it took only a second or two for the scribbling to commence. After reading the words she wrote, Black deemed them "too profane to be published. It was the most sinful invocation for the condemnation of a fellow being's soul."

The newsman, however, was not yet finished. He next tapped on the door casing with a pencil and "the force" followed suit, mimicking the sounds. Black then tapped out Morse code, and again the force mimicked him. Dr. Carritte got into the act by whistling a snippet from an Irish ditty, and the unseen force kept time with him by tapping out the tune.

When the Teeds told Black that no attempt had ever been made to converse with the force, he explained to them that the tried and accepted method of holding a conversation with a knocking spirit was to ask it pointed questions and teach it to knock in answer: three raps meant "yes," two raps indicated that the spirit "didn't know," and one rap meant "no." Black then commenced to ask the force a series of questions. They were all answered by prompt and, in many cases, accurate knocks. Its willingness to be questioned, however, depended upon Black's location in the room. When he approached too near the wall where Esther was sitting and from which the rapping appeared to be coming, the responses were faint. When he touched the wall, they stopped altogether; when he moved away from it, they grew louder; and when he turned his back to them, they became "joyfully loud." Black asked the force how many people were in the room, how many were male, how many female, and how many of them were married. He reported to his astonished readers that all the responses to these enquiries were correct.

The force also rapped accurately when Black asked how many miles he had travelled to visit Esther that day and how many children Dr. Carritte had. Black tried to get it to spell its answers by going through the alphabet and having it knock when the appropriate letter was reached, another method commonly used in communication with spirits. This time, however, the force rapped at nearly every letter, rendering its answers meaningless. Black then asked Esther to go into the pantry once again and shut the door. Jennie, assured by the force that she would not be harmed, went into the pantry as well. The sounds now seemed to come through the pantry shelves as well as through the door. To test the girls, Dr. Carritte quickly opened the pantry door—he found Jennie and Esther standing quietly in the middle of the room. Black took his turn in the pantry with Esther but was disappointed that the ghost "obstinately refused to rap while he was in there though it is said to have been quite demonstrative on a previous evening when the editor of the *Amherst Gazette* was in the same place."

With their home well into the second month of strange noises, Esther's restless nights, the crowds, and the local press, Daniel and Olive decided that everyone needed a respite. On October 31, 1878, the *Chignecto Post* reported that "Miss Cox, the heroine of the mysterious manifestations that have created such a sensation at Amherst, the past two months, is now at Upper Sackville, stopping at Mr. Gideon Snowdon's. The manifestations have again ceased." Gideon Snowdon was the father-in-law of Esther's sister Nellie; Nellie and husband James were living with his parents. Esther stayed there for two weeks, resting, helping with the housework, and attending church. Whatever was tormenting the girl seems to have left her in peace for the duration of her Sackville visit. And all was quiet at 6 Princess Street in her absence.

In mid-November, when Esther returned to Amherst, she and Jennie were moved to another bedroom in an attempt to get a fresh start. Days later, however, Esther declared that she heard "a voice informing her that the house was to be set on fire that night. It also told her that it had once lived on earth, but had been dead for some years and was now only a ghost." Surprisingly, the rest of the family, after all they had been through, laughed at this warning. They should have known better. A few minutes later, a lit match fell from the ceiling onto the bed, and for the next ten minutes several more seemed to come out of mid-air and fall around the room, with everyone scrambling to extinguish the fires. Along with the matches, the loud sounds started up again. So now, just over two months after the first occurrence, the force had added fire to its arsenal and, through Esther, had identified itself as a ghost. Six Princess Street indeed seemed to be haunted.

During the following week two fires broke out in the Teed home, the first when one of Esther's dresses was rolled up under her bed and set on fire, and the second when a barrel of wood shavings stored in the cellar began to smoulder. Olive and Esther attempted to extinguish the flames in the cellar with pails of water but, unable to contain them on their own, ran out into the street screaming for help. Some neighbourhood men rushed in and put out the fire using one of Olive's parlour rugs.

A few days after this scare, the ghost struck again—this time in a whole new way.

John White, the owner and manager of a local restaurant, lived with his wife, Sarah, sons Frederick and Charles, and daughter Mary in downtown Amherst. John, one of the many locals keenly interested in the manifestations surrounding Esther, had become a regular at 6 Princess Street. One evening, just before retiring, the White family heard a knock at their front door. Opening it, John found a tired looking Daniel Teed standing there. Daniel told John he needed help. He had to get Esther out of the house right away or it would be burned to the ground.

The Teeds had just settled into the parlour for the evening when Esther suddenly let out a scream and pointed to a corner of the room, saying she could see a ghost. She described it as a "him" with "burning eyes" who laughed and said that if she did not leave the house right away he would set it on fire. The rest of the family could neither hear nor see this apparition, but the girl was clearly upset and they had taken her word for it. Daniel asked if it would be possible for Esther to stay with John and his family for a few days. The ghost had not followed her on her recent stay in Sackville, so it was unlikely it would show up at the Whites. After consulting with Sarah, John agreed to take Esther in. Off she went once again to seek refuge in another home and to give the Teed family a rest and some peace of mind.

At the Whites' home, Esther was a model guest helping with the housework and looking after the children. She also went to church, read her Bible, and mended and sewed. Happily, the ghost was nowhere to be seen or heard. After Esther had been with the Whites for about a month, however, her old nemesis caught up with her. One day, while she was scrubbing the front hall floor, the brush suddenly disappeared from her hand. She let out a cry that brought Sarah and daughter Mary to her aid. After looking high and low for the brush, the women were shocked to see it fall from the ceiling, narrowly missing Esther's head. After the brush incident, the ghost was back in business, behaving much as it had at the Teeds. The rapping and knocking started again, and Esther and the Whites carried on conversations with the ghost. John White recalled that it "could tell how much money people had in their pockets both by knocking on the floor or wall, or on a table or by telling Esther so that she could tell others." The family could also hear the ghost walking through the house. All this was bearable for the family until the fires started again. It was then that John White began taking Esther to work with him.

White's Oyster Saloon was located on Victoria Street, next to the Baptist Church and across the road from the post office and

Bird's Book Store. It was one of many establishments, popular throughout North America, that catered to the booming market for fresh oysters harvested by fishermen in the Maritimes—including at Wallace, Nova Scotia; Shediac, New Brunswick; and Malpeque, Prince Edward Island—and shipped to retailers throughout the region. The shellfish, considered a poor man's dish, was the basis of hearty meals at little cost. One could dine on oyster stew, scalloped oysters, or the ever-popular oyster on the half-shell.

In an *Amherst Gazette* advertisement, White enthused that he was "prepared to furnish refreshments with hot coffee, at all hours and oysters served in all styles." He also offered fruit, candy, and groceries at the "lowest cash prices." And, in November 1878, he had yet another attraction to offer his patrons: local celebrity Esther Cox was now waiting on customers, washing dishes, cleaning floors, and wreaking havoc at White's Oyster Saloon.

CHAPTER 3

Cashing In on the Great Amherst Mystery

> The Cox- electro- magnetic- dynamic- mesmeric- diabolic- hair lifting- thunder-pealing- chair dancing performances is again in operation, this time at White's Oyster Saloon, Amherst.
> ~ CHIGNECTO POST, DECEMBER 5, 1878

> We mention that case once more to protest against the wickedness of taking around a poor Nova Scotia girl as an object to be exhibited for so much money. The civil authorities ought to interfere.
> ~ PRESBYTERIAN WITNESS (HALIFAX), JUNE 1879

On December 5, 1878, the *Chignecto Post* ran a letter to the editor written by William Henry Rogers, the Inspector of Fisheries for Nova Scotia. Rogers, born in Pugwash, was a respected and well-known member of Amherst society, a beloved husband, and father of ten. He attended the Amherst Baptist Church and was an ardent temperance man who, to this end, wrote letters, delivered speeches, and established a temperance hotel in the town.

Rogers's letter recounted a recent experience he had had at White's Oyster Saloon. On December 4, he had entered the restaurant and been regaled by John White with stories of what had occurred just hours before. He wrote, "I hereby declare that Mr. White said to me, 'I wish you have been in a little sooner, I would have cured you of your unbelief in the manifestations caused by Miss Cox. We have had wonderful manifestations this afternoon, while she sat with her feet on the stove. The doors of it flew about at such a rate that I thought they would break; I fastened the oven door back against the box, with the axe-handle braced against the wall, when it flew off the hinges and fell on the floor.'"

Rogers went on to tell readers that he himself then attempted to put the oven door back in place. Esther was seated nearby, with her feet once again on the oven. Suddenly, the door, weighing about ten pounds, jumped off its hinges and fell to the floor. Esther, becoming frightened, moved to a stool in the centre of the kitchen. Distinct rapping sounds then could be heard coming from under the floor near where she sat. Rogers immediately began communicating with the sound. "Give one loud rap," he requested, and it was given instantly; "now two raps, now three." Seeing his commands obeyed, he then asked, "Who are you, anyway—the devil?" Three raps was the response. "Are you after Miss Cox?" Three raps. "So you want me, too?" One rap. "Are you a human being, and are you living?" were the next questions, both of which were answered by three raps. Rogers then whistled the tune to "Yankee Doodle," while the rappings kept time.

In the kitchen with Rogers that afternoon, along with Esther and John White, were Jennie Cox, the Reverend Dr. Clay, and Dr. Carritte, who now took up the questioning. "How many people are in this room?" the doctor wanted to know. Five raps was the immediate and distinct response. "How many in the next room?" While two or three people were there, the response was just one rap. Rogers noted that whenever Dr. Carritte touched Esther, holding her hand or placing his palm on the top of her head, the knocking would cease.

Rogers likely wrote this letter at the behest of John White, who wanted word of the manifestations to spread and to be seen as having the support of a solid and respected citizen. Rogers initially was a sceptic, but the events he wrote of apparently changed his mind. On December 8, Rogers wrote another letter, this time a private one to Dr. Clay in which he stated "the girl is honest and to be pitied. I wish she was in some more intelligent hands than she is." Whether he was referring to the Teeds, John White, or another individual cannot be known.

William Rogers was far from being the only one to observe Esther's manifestations, which now had left the confines of private homes and were making public appearances. Saloon visitors and patrons who came to gawk at the source of the Great Amherst Mystery were regaled, on a daily basis, by chairs and tables moving about, objects flying around the kitchen, and, of course, the ever-present knockings.

The ghostly entertainment at the oyster saloon, however, was not long lived. All at once, Esther became seriously ill. On December 12, the *Chignecto Post* reported that she had contracted diphtheria. Known in Europe as the "strangling angel of children," diphtheria was one of the nineteenth century's most dreaded and highly infectious diseases. Symptoms include a sore throat, fever, malaise, hoarseness, and difficulty in swallowing and breathing, all caused by bacteria that inflamed the respiratory tract, in particular, the throat. People often died of suffocation from the thick grey membranes that formed there. The skin could also be affected in the ear, eye, or genital area. Today we know that diphtheria is transmitted by airborne respiratory droplets and that overcrowding and poor living conditions can contribute to its spread. In the nineteenth century, however, it was thought to be caused by dirt and dampness in homes, drains, and cesspools. Today, diphtheria is prevented by immunization and treated with antibiotics, but in Esther's time, the so-called cures were complicated and highly ineffective. Homemade remedies such as powdered sulphur were believed to stop diphtheria in the same way as they cured the itch—by destroying the living agent that caused it. The powder was set on fire and the patient made to inhale the fumes. It was blown into children's throats through a quill or swallowed and used as a gargle by adults. It could also be taken by the teaspoon in a glass of water.

Usually, diphtheria cases were not commented upon in the newspapers unless to report a death or the illness of a prominent person. But Esther was a local celebrity, her every move a matter of comment, so her illness was news. Luckily, unlike so many others who contracted the disease at this time and died, Esther recovered. During her illness and recuperation she stayed at the Snowden home in Sackville, safely away from all the Teed and White children, and the ghost mercifully let her be.

While Esther was entertaining John White's customers and later lying in her sick bed, the Reverend Dr. Edwin Clay became the first to write about what was now known as the Amherst or Cox Mystery. By the end of November 1878, a mere three months after the start of the manifestations, Clay had turned his notes into a lecture and was ready to take to the road on a speaking tour. The *Colchester Sun*, a daily newspaper in Truro,

Nova Scotia, editorialized that Clay's statements about what he had witnessed at Daniel Teed's home and White's Oyster Saloon "strongly verify the reports that have come to us of something really inexplicable in this now celebrated case." The editorial ended with a plea: "cannot our YMCA or the Reform Club get the Dr. to give his promised lecture in Truro?" In December 1878, Clay, who lived part-time in Halifax and was employed as a Dominion immigration agent, was lecturing on the subject of Esther Cox throughout that city.

In January 1879, with Esther recovered and back at home with Daniel and Olive, the ghost returned to its mischief with renewed force. Chairs, tables, and other pieces of furniture moved about of their own accord, and the raps and knocking were louder than ever. The fires started up again as well. On several occasions, 6 Princess Street caught fire between the walls. Of all the puzzling manifestations of the Mystery, these fires were the most worrisome, and were becoming a concern for many Amherst citizens whose homes and businesses were nearby. In a crowded town centre filled with wooden buildings, it would not take long for a small fire to spread quickly and perhaps cause loss of life and property.

Esther told everyone that the ghost was responsible for this mischief, but the authorities were of another opinion entirely. On January 23, 1879, the *Chignecto Post* reported that Esther had recently been "placed in the charge of Mr. John Trenholm, the veteran constable." In nineteenth-century Canada, women prisoners, in the absence of adequate prison or jail facilities, were sometimes kept in the home of a constable or sheriff under the supervision of his wife. Although Amherst did have a jail, there is no record of Esther being either arrested at this time or living with the Trenholm family. She may have simply been placed under some sort of probation, perhaps having to report regularly to Trenholm, who would have been responsible for keeping her on her best behaviour.

However vigilant, Constable Trenholm could not control what happened in Esther's bedroom. During the night of January 26, Esther and Jennie once again screamed for help. They told the frazzled Daniel and Olive that they had seen Bob MacNeill's form hovering above their bed brandishing a knife and threatening them. On another evening, shortly after, as reported in the January 30 *Saint John Daily Telegraph*, Esther claimed that she heard the voice of Bob MacNeill saying, "if she will marry him the manifestations will cease." Esther was clearly still smitten with Bob and his whereabouts were obviously a matter of interest to the press as well. The *Daily Telegraph* went on to report that "sometime ago McNeill stopped a short time in Fairville, near St. John. He is now in Malagash, NS."

Esther, under whatever restrictions, if any, placed upon her by Constable Trenholm and the Amherst authorities, was soon travelling herself. In early March, she was in Saint John at the invitation of Dr. Aaron Alward. The one-time editor and proprietor of the *Temperance Telegram*, the voice of the Order of the Sons of Temperance, Dr. Alward had many interests and had held a number of political offices, including that of mayor of Saint John from 1866 to 1870. Dr. Carritte had once lived in the port city, and he and Alward were acquainted: both physicians had concurrently been members of the local Union Lodge of Masons. Dr. Alward may have become aware of Esther's troubles through the press—the *Saint John Daily Telegraph* often carried news reports about her. It is also likely that Dr. Carritte contacted Alward to talk about his most interesting patient and ask him for advice. In any case, Dr. Alward wanted to meet Esther.

Aaron Alward was just one of several men Esther met in Saint John who were interested in the occult sciences—astrology, alchemy, magic, and witchcraft—including businessman Alexander Christie, whose manufacturing company built doors, sashes, blinds, and mouldings; Amos Fales, a gilder and carver; master mariner James Beck; and a Mr. Ritchie.

Esther stayed with Captain James Beck and his wife, Ellen, in their rented accommodations at 40 King's Square. Designed in 1848, King's Square was and remains the most prominent of Saint John's public spaces. Surrounded by residential and commercial buildings, King's Square was a bustling part of the port city. Walking around the neighbourhood with Mrs. Beck, Esther might have picked up sweets for her nephews at Thomas White's Confectionary, passed by Andrew Armstrong's cigar and spirit shop, and visited the Market Wharf to buy fresh fish for dinner. Esther's evening strolls in the square took place under the careful eye of Patrick Canning, the area's night watchman.

Esther saw a new and improved Saint John in the spring of 1879. Almost two years earlier, on June 20, 1877, in one of the most defining episodes in its history, the city had suffered a great fire. Believed to have started in Henry Fairweather's storehouse near today's Market Square, the fire razed about 80 hectares of the city, destroying 1,612 structures. When Esther visited Saint John, more than 90 percent of the city had been rebuilt, the rubble replaced with larger, more substantial buildings, many of them brick. New building codes and wider streets made the possibility of a fire much less likely or devastating.

On March 28, 1879, Esther's nineteenth birthday, the *Amherst Gazette* reported that she "had gone to visit relatives in the State of Maine." Her father, Archibald, his wife, Ann, and her stepbrothers still lived there. If she did indeed make the journey to

Maine, it would have been the first time in many years that she had seen her father. Besides the mention in the *Gazette*, however, there is no other reference to the Maine trip. The journey to the States may have been the story told to any reporters who came around 6 Princess Street during her absence, to put them off the scent of Esther's Saint John visit. There is certainly no reference to it in any of the local papers, and Esther's whereabouts in early 1879 was a hot topic in news items and editorials in the Maritime region. If it had been known that Esther was in Saint John, it undoubtedly would have been reported. Esther's Saint John hosts may have wanted to keep their interest in the infamous girl quiet. They might have feared that their reputations as community leaders and prominent citizens would be tarnished if their interest in the occult sciences was generally known.

Whether Esther visited Maine or not, soon after her return to Amherst she received another invitation. John Van Amburgh and his wife owned a farm about two and a half miles outside of town and, seemingly not bothered by her infamy or behaviour, asked Esther to visit them. John Van Amburgh, at age fifty, was a retired sailor. He, his wife and children, and elderly mother lived on the farm. Esther stayed with the family for two months, doing housework and tending the children. During her stay, a few knockings were heard but, on the whole, her life there was quiet. However, Esther was still being watched by the newspapers. On May 7, the *Amherst Gazette* reported on her ability to bring sounds from a cabinet organ by merely pressing the keys, without having to supply air to the bellows. Such a phenomenon was seen, by the press and the "several reliable witnesses" who were with her, as proof of her power.

Esther, however, soon became bored at the isolated Van Amburgh farm and, after eight weeks, returned to Amherst, reportedly "having become weary of the dull life she was compelled to lead in the woods." She returned to 6 Princess Street and the employ of John White.

Soon after coming home this time, Esther Cox met the man who was to ensure that she would become a household name and that her story would be remembered into the twenty-first century. That man was Walter Hubbell.

Between 1857 and 1880, Saint John native and impresario William Nannary was a prominent figure in the theatre world in the Maritime provinces. His company, the Atlantic Victorian Theatre, based in Saint John, featured an ever-changing line-up of performers who travelled to Halifax, St. John's (Newfoundland), Moncton, Charlottetown, Ottawa, Maine, and smaller communities such as Amherst, performing scenes from Shakespearean plays, romantic comedies, and modern dramas. Nannary also managed companies at the Academy of Music in both Halifax and Saint John. In his attempt to move from amateur to professional theatre, Nannary periodically hired minor actors from Boston and New York to come to the Maritime provinces to perform as headliners alongside the local talent. It was their moment to be stars and to bask in the limelight. Walter Hubbell was one of these actors.

Hubbell's home base was New York City. In January 1879, he travelled from there to Halifax at the behest of his agent, who had secured him winter employment with Nannary's troupe. The Atlantic Victorian Theatre was in Halifax from January 14 until March 31 and produced thirty-seven plays, including *The Romance of a Poor Man*, which opened to large audiences. It

Walter Hubbell years after the Great Amherst Mystery.

was during his time in Halifax that the twenty-eight-year-old Hubbell read about the Great Amherst Mystery in local newspapers. He immediately saw it as his opportunity, as he explained later, to "expose the mystery, and make money out of it while so doing."

Walter Hubbell was a shameless self-promoter with a strong sense of his own abilities, both on and off the stage. He felt that he, and he alone, could solve the mystery of Esther Cox. He considered himself qualified for such a task due to his experience as an actor and his familiarity with "all those mechanical devices which we use upon the stage for the presentation of illusive effects so often the wonder and admiration of the public." Hubbell also fancied himself an expert in fraud detection. He writes that in 1872 an unscrupulous practitioner of "modern spiritualism" was taking advantage of a friend, systemically fleecing her of her life savings while declaring his ability to channel her deceased mother. Hubbell claims that he uncovered this imposter for the charlatan he was, and that this was just one of many episodes in which he was "successful in exposing a number of so-called mediums."

Walter Hubbell was born in Philadelphia on April 26, 1851. A writer as well as an actor, one of his many books was a *History of the Hubbell Family*, in which his pride in his lineage is evident. His great-grandfather Silas Hubbell was a captain in the Revolutionary War. According to Walter, he dumped tea into Boston Harbor and fought with General Washington and at Bunker Hill. His son, Hubbell's grandfather Truman Mallory Hubbell—a Massachusetts cotton dealer, friend of James Fenimore Cooper, and expert marksman—was hailed as the inspiration for Natty Bumppo of the Leather Stocking Series, which includes *The Last of the Mohicans*. Walter's father, William, studied law and in 1850 was appointed as an attorney to the U.S. Supreme Court. An inventor, he created the explosive shell fuses used by the U.S. army and navy during the Civil War.

Walter Hubbell claimed he had been on the stage since boyhood and "played every line of parts in the classic and standard drama," acting beside a variety of well-known British and American performers, including the notorious Charlotte Cushman and Edwin Booth, who was considered by many to be the greatest actor of the nineteenth century and brother to the assassin John Wilkes Booth.

Hubbell's first step toward solving what he coined the "Great Amherst Mystery" was to write to John White, while still in Halifax, suggesting a partnership in which the two of them would exhibit Esther throughout Canada and the United States. Hubbell himself would accompany the girl and explain the Mystery to rapt audiences. White answered Hubbell's letter in the affirmative and shortly afterward began to promote the event. In the first week of March 1879, both the *Moncton Daily Times* and the *Saint John Daily Telegraph* told their readers that "Esther Cox is to be exhibited."

Putting a person like Esther, considered both a celebrity and a curiosity, on display and attempting to draw a paying audience was common practice before the days of radio and television. Travelling entertainments, whether their message was sacred or secular, comical or serious, were considered by some as edifying relief from hard work and lack of variety, but by others as sensational and ungodly. Audiences nevertheless flocked to hear and see them. Lectures, like those delivered by author Oscar Wilde and social reformer Henry Ward Beecher, music recitals, magic lantern shows, performances by magicians, mediums, and marvels like tiny Tom Thumb played to packed churches, theatres, and town halls throughout North America. The Maritimes and Newfoundland were no exceptions. Barely a week went by in the region's larger towns and villages that did not include such performances, the more sensational the better. To a show-business veteran like Walter

Hubbell, Esther Cox and her notoriety seemed a natural for the travelling entertainment circuit.

While Esther was in Saint John, Hubbell and the rest of Nannary's troupe had engagements in Amherst, performing on March 25 and 26, and in Moncton at Ruddick's Hall on March 27, 28, and 29. *The Marble Heart* and skits by comedian Walter Lennox were well received. During his stay in Amherst, Hubbell visited the Teed home and met Olive Teed, who informed him that all was quiet at the house since the ghost had followed Esther to Saint John. Hubbell and White then apprised Olive of their plans to exhibit Esther throughout North America.

Unfortunately for them, Hubbell and White were not able to carry out their scheme until June. Hubbell was still under contract with Nannary and needed to go to Newfoundland with the troupe to fulfill his obligations. We learn what they had in mind for Esther and of White's frustration to get started with it in a letter he wrote to Hubbell on April 16, 1879. It appears that the actor and the businessman were not the only ones to see the money-making potential in Esther Cox:

> *Dear Sir: I thought that I would write and let you no [know] now that a fair that we were talking about is giting along the girl is back to Amherst in my Charge and is engaged to go with us every thing is working well so far all right. I wish you were here so we could git away I fel that we are loosing time the manifestations is still going on yet I wish you could come back and leave them behind but I suppose that cant bee so I will have to wait till you return with the rest I think it would not bee a bad play to go to Halifax firs but I*

> will leave that to you please lett me here from you as soon as you can for I will bee very ancues [anxious] to here from you there is other perties [parties] is tring to get her she sais she will not go with them.
>
> Yours J. W. White

Although the road show was on hold for the time being, things were hopping at White's Oyster Saloon. On the evening of May 6, Esther met John White's son-in-law, Robert Hutchinson, on the sidewalk near the saloon. She had just closed up for a while, she told him, in order to go for tea, when, while crossing the street, she heard a loud noise coming from the building. She was too afraid to go back on her own and investigate, and asked Hutchinson to accompany her. They found the saloon kitchen in a state of disarray. Three earthenware bowls that had been left top down on a table to dry were now facing upwards. One of them contained a twenty-pound teakettle, the other a coffeepot. Basins still containing water had been moved about and a cooking pot had left its shelf and come to rest on the table with the bowls.

The mischief continued later on that week. Esther told reporters that, while in the midst of washing window blinds in the saloon kitchen, she had left the room for a minute and upon her return found that they had been removed from the tub and thrown onto the coal bin located in the corner of the room. She had had to clean the blinds all over again. The *Amherst Gazette* noted that this was not the kind of joke that a "washerwoman would be fond of perpetrating on herself." A week later, on May 16, the *Gazette* announced "Her life Endangered by Flying Missiles—Assassinated with a knife." The article was accompanied by a line drawing of the saloon kitchen that provided the location of the kitchen's cupboards, work tables, stove, and doorways.

Chignecto Post editor J. Albert Black often visited White's establishment to check up on the progress of the Mystery. One day, Esther was washing dishes at the washstand, with the newsman stationed just outside the kitchen door, when the ghosts struck again. A water glass fell and broke a large earthenware bowl. Esther said that the glass had moved through the air on its own accord from the cupboard, which was seven feet away. On hearing the crash, Black, along with Robert Hutchinson and others, ran into the kitchen. They verified that Esther had never moved from her position by the washstand. A minute or two later, all witnessed the glass moving once again. This time, it flew over Esther's head and shattered in the far corner. Esther and John White told Black of other occasions when a bar of soap and metal scale weights had flown around the room of their own volition, while a wash basin, sitting on a small table, suddenly had come down from its perch and moved along the floor of its own accord, following Esther as she passed by.

The *Gazette* reported on another, more disturbing incident at John White's place of business. White's thirteen-year-old son Fred was in the kitchen whittling while Esther worked nearby. Suddenly, his knife was "taken from his hand by the devilish ghost who instantly stabbed Esther in the back with it, leaving the knife sticking in the wound, which was bleeding profusely." Fred hurriedly extracted the knife from the poor girl's back, closed it up, and placed it in his pocket. He had no sooner done that when "the ghost obtained possession of it again and, as quick as a flash of lightning stuck it into the same wound." Fred took the knife from Esther's bleeding back once again, placed it in the cash drawer, locked it, and put the key in his pocket. There is no indication that these wounds were tended to by a doctor.

The spirit was also flexing its muscles at the White residence, where Esther was once again staying. She was sitting in the kitchen when a glass bottle came down from the pantry shelf, hurled across the kitchen floor, and smashed into pieces against the wall. On another occasion, when Esther walked into the coal shed, Sarah White witnessed large clumps of coal flying about, and a visitor to the White home claimed that she saw a broom leave the front door area where Esther had placed it and settle on a woodpile eighteen feet away.

Esther moved back to Daniel Teed's house in May 1879, where the ghost was soon up to its old tricks once again. Baby George was sleeping in his cradle when all at once he was lifted bodily and placed gently on the floor. Later that day, both cradle and baby were tipped over. The intrigued Robert Hutchison, while visiting 6 Princess Street, saw a salt cellar go through the air and smash against a door frame eight feet away. Hutchison, noting later on that "nothing moves while the eye is fixed on it," was determined to keep a close watch on a comb that lay on the table before him. Unfortunately, he happened to look elsewhere just for a moment when the comb took flight to the ceiling and then fell to the floor.

By the second week of June, Walter Hubbell was back in Halifax and ready to start his new career as stage manager of the Great Amherst Mystery. He travelled to Amherst by rail on June 11, and he met once again with the anxious John White. After a meal at the saloon, they walked to 6 Princess Street, where Esther and Hubbell finally met.

Esther informed the actor that there were now six ghosts in her life that had made their names known to her, and she claimed she could see and hear them all. She described their appearance as "like living shadows of men and women." Besides the original ghost, whose name was Bob Nickle and who was the ringleader of the group, she was now being followed by the spirits of Bob's sister Jane, Eliza MacNeill, Peter Teed, and sisters Maggie and Mary Fisher. Bob and Maggie were the most dominant personalities of the six spirits, and Esther assured Hubbell that they both agreed she could take part in the exhibition tour.

Hubbell spent the afternoon of June 11 with John White, Esther, and Olive listening to their stories, and although he was not yet convinced of the presence of any supernatural powers, he declared himself, nevertheless, quite prepared to "write a lecture from what the family told me of the affair and what I could hear from newspaper reports and to deliver it with proper effect." Hubbell was sure that what he called Esther's "tremendous reputation" would draw in large audiences and make it worth his while financially.

Hubbell and White returned to the Teed home later that evening, and the actor was introduced to Daniel, Jennie, and Neander Quigley, a family friend. They invited Hubbell to take part in a seance and to hear the ghosts in action. The entertainment began with sounds of scratching, rapping, knockings, and the tipping of the table. Hubbell described the scratching sound like that of "invisible human finger nails," while the knocking was like "dull sounds produced by the hands as they rubbed the table and struck it with invisible clenched fists." Esther told Hubbell that the spirits of Bob Nickle and Maggie Fisher were both present, and invited him to question them. Hubbell asked them to recite the numbers of his watch, which they did. He also asked them to tell him the time as displayed on the dining room clock and the date of a coin in his pocket, both of which were also answered correctly. Hubbell then whistled "Yankee Doodle" and was accompanied by knocking. Hubbell noted that he had "watched all the people present, saw their hands and feet by the light of the coal-oil lamp in the room" and detected no signs of trickery among the group. He and White left the Teed home at eleven o'clock that night, ready to take the show on the road.

They lost no time. The next day, June 12, Hubbell, White, and Esther left Amherst around noon by train for Moncton. A large crowd gathered at the station to see them off. While Hubbell and White originally had big plans of starting the show in Halifax and taking it from there to Boston, they opted for first testing the waters closer to home. During the train ride, while Esther gazed out the window, and White talked of how successful the trip would be, Hubbell polished the lecture he had started earlier in the day.

In Moncton, they booked into the American House on Main Street. Earlier that year, the *Daily Times* had run an advertisement paid for by proprietor W. R. Baggs, which announced that the American House, formerly the Queen's Hotel, had "recently being thoroughly repaired, re-fitted and re-furnished for the accommodation of permanent and transient boarders." The guest house had coaches on hand that were available to meet all trains and carry passengers to and from the hotel at no charge. Potential customers could rest assured that "no pains will be spared to accommodate guests and promote their comfort." It is likely that Hubbell, during his recent visit to Moncton with Nannary's troupe, had lodged at the American House and suggested it to White as a suitable place to stay while in town.

John White had secured two shows at Ruddick's Hall for the following Friday and Saturday evenings. The June 13 edition of the *Daily Times* heralded their arrival, noting that "Esther Cox, the heroine of the 'Amherst Mystery' is billed for Ruddick's Hall to-night" and that, as was proper, she was "escorted by a guardian or manager." Ruddick's Hall, a former Methodist Church, was also located on Moncton's Main Street. Opened by Andrew Ruddick just the previous year, it was available for a $2-per-day rental fee to respectable parties. It was a popular venue for a variety of live entertainments, musical concerts, plays, lectures, and once even a perjury trial so notorious that the Moncton courthouse could not contain all the onlookers. Again, Hubbell would have been familiar with this venue, having himself been on the stage there recently.

Esther, Hubbell, and White had settled nicely into their lodging house and were resting in the parlour when one of the ghosts caused a large rocking chair to move back and forth while Esther sat about fifteen feet from it. Hubbell hoped that the ghosts would be as willing to perform the next night when he and Esther were on the Ruddick Hall stage. He planned to stand at a podium, explaining the phenomenon to a baffled and appreciative audience while Esther sat on his right and the ghosts wreaked havoc in the hall, moving items and making loud rapping and knocking sounds. It was his intention, he said, "to give three lectures a week, hoping that the ghosts would know and move objects on the stage."

It was not to be. On both evenings, while Hubbell pontificated about the Mystery, the ghosts refused to present themselves in any capacity, and Esther sat, silent, holding a fan to hide behind in case, due to nerves and stage fright, she started to laugh. Immediately after the Saturday show, Hubbell left Moncton for Chatham, New Brunswick, which was to be their next stop, while Esther and John White stayed behind.

As if to make up for their absence at Ruddick's Hall, the ghosts put on a show during Sunday morning services at the First Moncton Baptist Church. The June 18 edition of the *Moncton Dispatch* reported that "during the first singing, the ghost manifested itself by knocking, apparently on the floor of the pew in front. When told to stop by Miss Cox, it would cease the noise for a moment, but then it would break out worse than ever. Throughout the prayer it continued; but when the organ began for the second singing, the noise became so distinct and disturbing that Miss Cox and party were forced to leave the church." Esther, on returning to their rooms at the American House, immediately became ill. She was confined to bed for the rest of the day in great pain while also suffering from hiccoughs, a rapid heartbeat, and swelling to parts of her body. The doctor who was called to her bedside told reporters that her symptoms were caused by "nervous excitement."

By Monday afternoon Esther had recovered fully, and the ghosts commenced their stunts once more. Esther told the *Dispatch* that "while she was sitting by the window of a room on the ground floor, a fan dropped out of the window; she went outside to recover it and on returning, a chair from the opposite side of the room was found upside down near the door, as though it had attempted to follow her out of the room." Later, while she was writing a letter to her sister Nellie, she claimed that "the ghost took possession of the pen, and wrote in a different hand altogether," and that she was "able to look in another direction and not show the least interest in what the pen was writing" while the scribbling continued. That evening Esther once again suffered at the hands of the ghosts, much the same as she had the night before, but the next morning she was fine once again. The *Dispatch* ended its article with the observation that, "if the ghost is willing, Miss Cox will leave for Chatham by train today."

While the daily newspapers were obviously delighting in the spectacle of the road trip, other literary vehicles cast Esther as a victim of greed and crassness. The *Presbyterian Witness and Evangelical Advocate*, the newspaper of the Presbyterian Church in Nova Scotia, and the *Wesleyan*, the voice of the Methodist Church, both published in Halifax, spoke out about the unsuitableness of the whole affair. The *Witness* pointed the finger at the secular press for fanning the flames of interest in the case, stating:

> [T]he newspapers are greatly to blame for "working up" this pitiable sensation. The story is now going the rounds that the girl, Esther Cox, is to be taken around on exhibition. In the name of humanity, propriety, religion and decency, we earnestly protest against a proceeding so base and disgusting. If the girl is sick why should her infirmities be exhibited to the public? We protest against the wickedness of taking around a poor Nova Scotia girl as an object to be exhibited for so much money. The civil authorities ought to interfere.

The *Wesleyan* concentrated on the inappropriateness of placing a woman on public display:

> After passing through an extraordinary career of mystery, Esther Cox is to be as a scientific phenomenon. Surely if her "visitations" have been an affliction, as it was affirmed, this last indignity ought not to be

> added. It is sufficient humiliation for humanity to endure the rhapsodies which are uttered as an assumed explanation of this girl's condition without pointing to her in public as a being distinct from the rest of human kind. Besides, there are peculiarities in her case, if we hear the truth, which cannot be explained in a mixed audience. We advise that either the case be submitted to science absolutely, or Miss Cox be permitted to retain her womanly instincts by keeping in retirement.

Later, Hubbell would blame the deviousness of a man who had wanted to exhibit Esther himself as the reason behind this negative publicity. Despite these protestations from the religious community, no one else stepped in to question or halt the proceedings, and Esther and John White continued on their way. They departed Moncton on June 18 to meet up with Hubbell and perform on June 20 in the Chatham Masonic Hall, the venue of much of Chatham's entertainments. Fundraising teas, literary evenings, singing, and instrumental music, sometimes with a thirteen-piece orchestra, were all offered there in the months leading up to Esther's arrival.

She had two days to look around Chatham, a lumbering and shipbuilding community of between three and four thousand souls located along the south bank of the Miramichi River. Since the Intercolonial Railway did not pass through Chatham in 1879, the Hubbell party travelled directly to Newcastle, across the river, and from there took a carriage the rest of the way. White had secured accommodations at a boarding house run by a Mrs. Carroll, and the three travellers settled in to prepare for their northeastern New Brunswick debut.

Leading up to the Chatham show, the ghosts, as they had done before the presentation in Moncton, assured Hubbell, via Esther, that they would "move objects about while we were on stage in presence of an audience." Hubbell hoped it would be so, although he covered himself by stating that he "only advertised to give a complete account of the manifestations that had occurred, not those that would or might occur, not knowing whether the ghosts would keep their promise or not."

Hubbell's little troupe soon found that the Chatham audiences expected more for their money than did those in Moncton. They did not cotton to the idea of sitting for over an hour listening to Hubbell drone on about what the ghosts had done. They wanted to see some of that action on stage, and were not averse to showing their disappointment when it was not provided. After the presentation ended, again with no appearance from the ghosts, Esther rose from her chair, bowed as she had been taught by Hubbell, and the curtain was brought down. A few minutes later, she and Hubbell could hear shouting in the hall and noticed that White was taking a long time to get backstage with the night's proceeds. He eventually did appear with the news that a "ruffian had attempted to strike him." On hearing this, Hubbell's first thoughts were for the bottom line. He asked White if "he had our share of the receipts of the lecture, he replied in the affirmative and gave me the money, which I put it in my pocket." Hubbell instructed White to stay at the hall until he got Esther safely back to their rooming house. In a scene reminiscent of a snake oil salesman being run out of town on a rail, Hubbell and Esther were escorted to their lodgings by what he described as "a howling mob which threw stones and brick-bats at us."

Though they got away unharmed, Esther was, according to Hubbell, "entirely unnerved by the incident." Meanwhile, John

White decided to wash his hands of the whole matter. He was responsible for Esther's well-being and was afraid that they might come to physical harm if they put on another performance. He wanted to return to Amherst, and announced to Hubbell that he was done with show business. The trio left Chatham immediately, taking the midnight train to Amherst. They arrived home early the next day, June 21, a mere nine days after starting out on what Hubbell and White had believed would be a successful financial venture.

While John White quietly went back to managing his oyster saloon, the quick-thinking and ever-resourceful Hubbell already had a new plan. He asked the long-suffering Olive if he could board at 6 Princess Street over the summer. There was room for him, since both John Teed and William Cox had, months earlier, moved elsewhere. Hubbell was just as determined as ever to study the spirits that surrounded Esther, and now he saw another way in which to make money from this research. He would write a book.

CHAPTER 4

Living Among Spirits

The case has lately been watched closely by Mr. Walter Hubbell, who has determined to spend some time in its investigation.
~ THE BANNER OF LIGHT (BOSTON) JULY 12, 1879

The newest resident of 6 Princess Street was barely in the door when his research got off to a flying start. Hubbell had just settled into a comfortable chair in the parlour when the umbrella he had left in the dining room flew over his head. It was closely followed by a carving knife that whizzed through the air. He immediately investigated the pantry, from which the knife had come, and, finding no one there, knew that the ghosts were up to their old tricks once again. Hubbell returned to the parlour. Suddenly, the satchel that was resting on the floor beside his chair flew across the room, and a large chair moved rapidly towards him, ramming into the one on which he was seated.

It was at this point that Hubbell became a firm believer in the Amherst Mystery. Initially, he had taken Esther Cox for a fraud, a trickster. Now, after witnessing the unexplainable movement of these inanimate objects, he was "convinced that there is an invisible power within the atmosphere that men have so far failed to comprehend." Manifestations of the Mystery continued throughout the day. When Hubbell again entered the parlour, chairs, seven in all, fell over on their sides and a heavy glass paperweight flew through the air, nearly striking him on the head as he reclined on the couch with his face turned away. Hubbell relates that this particular incident made him feel "that I had escaped a most unnatural death. Truly in the haunted house murder lurked within the atmosphere." But more was yet to come. Later in the evening, while Esther was rocking baby George, a shoe came off the child's foot, travelled through the air and struck Hubbell behind his right ear. And this was just his first day as guest of Esther and the ghosts.

Hubbell woke up the next morning, June 22, eager for more manifestations. He was informed, however, that the ghosts rarely showed themselves on a Sunday. It truly was a day of rest for all. Hubbell admits that he was baffled as to why the ghosts refrained from their mischief on the Sabbath, claiming, "I never could ascertain reason, or assign one that was in accordance with the facts of the case."

But he did not have long to wait for the ghosts to show themselves again. Next morning, during breakfast, the sugar bowl lid fell to the floor and disappeared from view. After much searching by Olive, Esther, and Hubbell, they saw it fall from the ceiling. Table knives were hurled to the floor, the chairs once again fell over, the dining room table flipped over on its side and the floor rugs started sliding about. Hubbell saw "the whole room literally turned into a pandemonium, so filled with dust that I went into the parlor." But he was no safer there. He had just seated himself when a flower pot moved, on its own accord, from the window ledge to the centre of the room. A few seconds later, a bucket of water travelled through the air and came to rest beside the plant. And the marvels did not cease throughout the day. As Hubbell recorded in his journal, "a large empty sink stand and two empty bottles" were thrown at him, knitting needles taken from Esther's hands became missiles and three times the piece of cake that little George was trying to eat was snatched away and it too was lobbed at the visitor. George's clothes were also repeatedly torn from his body. Hubbell believed that the infant and the family cat were the only ones, besides Esther herself, able to see the ghosts. He noted that the baby "on more than one occasion, acted as if strangers were present whom he feared." That same day Esther's face was also slapped, the noise resounding through the Teed home and leaving "marks of fingers."

Later that afternoon, the spirits became more threatening: in an upstairs room, newspapers were set on fire. Hubbell reports that he believed the spirit "shoemaker Bob" was responsible for this and other fires. "Bob" would go around the house gathering combustible material, roll it up in a ball and "hide it in a basket of soiled linen or in a closet, then go and steal matches out of the match box in the kitchen" or from somebody's pocket. He would then light a fire, sometimes whispering to Esther where it was located; other times he taunted her with the fact that a fire had been set. The family would then run through the house carrying buckets of water, following the smell of smoke. Hubbell felt that this constant fire threat by "Bob the demon and fire fiend" was "the most truly awful calamity that could possibly befall any family, infidel or Christian, that could be conceived in the mind of man or ghost." He admired the fortitude of Olive Teed, a God-fearing woman, when she assured him that all would be well one day as "God was stronger than the Devil."

In the following days, Hubbell was able to document many more incidents for his research. The sugar bowl lid continued to vanish and reappear every morning at breakfast, and it was not the only item that played hide and go seek. Hubbell reports that, almost daily, articles would disappear and reappear, many of them taken from locked trunks and closets. The dining room table continued to be turned over and knocked upon. Thumping on the walls and floors was also a way for the "demon Bob" and his cohorts to communicate with the living. During his stay at 6 Princess Street, Hubbell reports he was in almost daily conversations with the spirits. Bob would converse by "pounding under the bay-window and on the floor of the room as if he had a blacksmith's hammer weighing fifty pounds." When asked if they were in heaven, the ghosts, by knocking, answered "No." When asked if they were in hell, they assured Hubbell that, indeed, that was where they were and when queried if they had seen the Devil, they replied in the affirmative with "the loudest kind of sledge hammer blows upon the floor."

One day, Esther was writing a letter to her sister Nellie when her hand was suddenly overpowered and "compelled to write '...Damn your soul to hell! God damn Hubbell's soul to hell and yours!'" Hubbell was furious at this and "cursed them in return, commanding them to go back to hell and cease tormenting Esther and her family." The spirits responded by throwing a bottle of ink on the carpet.

The mayhem continued all during Hubbell's first week of lodging at the Teeds. More knives were thrown about, more fires set. Hubbell, growing familiar with the tormenting spirits, routinely cursed them, but to no avail. Esther informed Hubbell that often while he and Bob were exchanging curses, Maggie Fisher whispered to her. But far worse was to come. Towards the end of the week, the ghosts added yet more physical abuse to their arsenal.

On the morning of June 26, Esther and Jennie informed Hubbell that during the night Bob had stuck them both with pins. They claimed he had marked them from head to toe with crosses, and they showed the actor the "bloody marks, scratched upon their hands, necks and arms" that had been left behind. This continued throughout the day. Hubbell writes that he was "kept busy pulling pins out of Esther, they came out of the air from all quarters, and were stuck into all the exposed portions of her person even her head, and inside of her ears." In all Hubbell pulled thirty pins out of the tormented girl.

Esther was continuously assaulted during Hubbell's residence in the house. He reported that, among other horrors, she received a triangular cut on her forehead with a steak bone, and an attempt was made to cut her throat with a carving knife. The spirit Maggie Fisher tried to slash her throat with a pair of shears, and she was also stabbed in the head with a fork.

Hubbell, too, had nocturnal visitors to his bedroom. One morning he reported that during the night Maggie Fisher "took quite an interest in me," knocking on the headboard of the bed and the nearby wall. He says they carried on a "most interesting conversation" by knocking out questions and answers to each other. Indeed, during Hubbell's stay with the Teeds, he and the spirit Bob slowly developed something of a friendship. Often Hubbell would request a match to start his pipe and a lit one would conveniently appear out of thin air.

All the while, the local press maintained its interest in Esther and stayed in regular contact with the Teed family. On June 26, the *Daily Times* of Moncton reported that "Esther Cox, not having proved a success on the stage; she still has manifestations to select audiences." The same week, the *Chignecto Post* and *Saint John Daily Telegraph* told their readers that "Esther

Cox has returned to Amherst after her short tour. Her health is better." By this time Hubbell himself was contacting the press about the goings on. The *Amherst Gazette* reported on June 27 that the case of Esther Cox "has lately been watched closely by Mr. Walter Hubbell, of Philadelphia, Penn. who has seen similar phenomena, and has determined to spend some time in its investigation. He has frequently caught bogus 'mediums' in their deceptions, and considers that Miss Cox could not easily deceive him if she were inclined to do so."

Hubbell was also communicating with newspapers farther afield. *The Banner of Light,* a popular spiritualist magazine out of Boston, reported on July 12, 1879, that its editors had received a letter from the actor on the progress of the Mystery. While the manifestations occurring in Esther's bedroom might take place at any time, on any night, it was a different story downstairs, Hubbell informed them, where the spirits not only observed the Sabbath as the day of rest, but also seemed to keep strict hours during the remainder of the week. Each day "the spirit manifestations commence about 8 pm and continue until 12 pm recommence about 1:30 pm and cease about 6 pm."

As the summer progressed, Esther's spirit companions continued to entertain and shock Hubbell. On one occasion, the sound of a trumpet was heard through the house. At the end of the day the noisemaker fell from the ceiling, but the family was at a loss to explain to whom it belonged or from where it came. Hubbell continued to have a variety of household objects and tools, in one instance a screwdriver, thrown at him.

Sometimes, though, the spirits were more social and accommodating. Once, when Hubbell, Esther, and Jennie were seated in the parlour, they made a game of having the spirits carry items to them from other parts of the house: "a fresh egg from the kitchen, a shaving brush from Daniel's room, two spools of cotton from Mrs. Teed's work-basket in the sewing room and a large number of hairpins from the girls' room." The female spirits were apparently not immune to the lure of pretty things. One day Esther, "after much hesitancy and blushing," told Hubbell that Maggie Fisher had taken a pair of black and white striped stockings from a bureau drawer and was wearing them. Esther could see them below the spirit's clothing. Hubbell was "astonished beyond expression at such information" and ordered Maggie to return Esther's stockings at once. The spirit obviously heard the command, as suddenly the stockings reappeared, falling down from the ceiling.

Hubbell frequently studied Esther to ascertain her powers of mind control by having her concentrate on an object so that it might move about under her direct power. He observed, however, that "the object her mind was fixed on would remain stationary, and something else would be moved that she had not even thought of, very often being brought from another room." Hubbell also tried an experiment to help him gauge the amount of electrical power or magnetism Esther held in her body. While both were seated in the Teed parlour, Hubbell asked Esther to place her hands in his and to look him squarely in the eye. Hubbell remembered, "I could distinctly feel a power like a current of electricity passing through my arms." As the experiment continued, the actor felt himself getting physically weak and sleepy while the girl felt no change to her system. After releasing Esther, Hubbell found that he was so depleted of energy he had to retire to bed and proceeded to sleep for twelve hours.

One night in July, Hubbell was awakened by Daniel so that he could see for himself what, up to that point, he had only heard about. Hubbell entered the girls' bedroom to find Esther swollen and writhing on the bed "as if Beelzebub was in her." Between crying and gasping for breath, Esther cried out, "Oh God! I wish I were dead! I wish I were dead!" Daniel and Hubbell tried to hold the girl down and to calm her but to no avail. The ghostly torment lasted for about three hours until poor Esther sank into a weakened state of exhaustion and finally sleep. On another evening her symptoms worsened. Esther appeared to be in a trance, lying on her back, her body rigid. Hubbell described her eyes as "set like a dying woman." While not conscious of anyone or anything around her, Esther sang hymns and said she was conversing with her deceased mother. She also reported that she spoke with people whom Daniel and Olive knew had once lived in Amherst but who had passed away before Esther moved there. Hubbell reported that he also asked her if she had seen any of his dead departed friends, but she had not. "This," he said, "all occurred while the Bible was under her pillow."

While Esther was Hubbell's first concern during his stay in Amherst, he also took part in community activities. He regularly attended meetings of the local reform club and was once asked to speak to the group about temperance. He recalled, "of course I spoke, and thanked God I was not a drunkard, but was never asked to speak again." Hubbell also went to Sunday services, usually joining Jennie at Christ Church to hear the Reverend Canon George Townshend. Only once did he and Esther together accompany the Teeds to the Methodist church, where "Bob the demon" behaved so badly that they were forced to leave. Any time the Reverend Temple mentioned Satan or the Holy Ghost, "Bob" would "knock on the floor or the back of the pew." When "Bob" began to throw the hymn books about and "upset the kneeling-stool," it was time for Hubbell and the embarrassed Esther to vacate the church.

Amherst Methodist Church, circa 1895.

By the latter part of July, Hubbell had been at the Teeds' home for about a month and the household had been in a constant uproar the whole time. The walls and woodwork were covered with burn marks from fires and gouges from furniture and other household items having been thrown against them. The doors were marred by knife cuts. Chairs and tables bore the marks of being thrown about. Enough was enough. In the last week of July, Daniel received a stern warning from his new landlord, James Bliss, a local magistrate, who, less than a year before, in December 1878, had purchased the property at 6 Princess Street.

Bliss told Daniel in no uncertain terms that Esther must leave the premises at once. He could not help but know what was going on in his house, what with the newspaper reports and the gossip from the street and White's Oyster Saloon about his infamous tenant, and he did not want his investment destroyed. So once again, the Teeds and Esther had no alternative but to find her another place to live. They contacted the Van Amburghs, who agreed to let Esther stay with them once more. She kissed her sisters and nephews goodbye and shook hands with Daniel and Hubbell, who later exclaimed, "Poor Esther! I shall never forget her. Such resignation. She was indeed a martyr."

Since Esther was leaving, Hubbell had no choice but to go as well. But with more than enough material for his book, he was satisfied and ready to move on. The last time Hubbell and Esther saw each other was on August 1, 1879. He stopped by the Van Amburgh farm to wish her well and remind her to be a "good girl." He found her working on a patchwork quilt and playing with her hosts' children. She told Hubbell that "she read her Bible every day, had not seen anything of the ghosts, and was consequently contented and happy." He returned to Amherst and that same afternoon met with W. S. Harkins, manager of a dramatic company who was getting an acting troupe together. Hubbell signed on with Harkins, and that night was on a train to Saint John to take part in another theatre production.

It took a while for Hubbell to be certain that he was safe from Bob, Maggie, and the rest of the spirits. He claimed that for months after he left Amherst, "any sudden sound would make me start and listen; but when I had become positive that the demons had not followed me, I became myself again."

Hubbell was nothing if not ambitious and industrious. Wasting no time, he worked the notes he had taken while at the Teeds into his book on the Great Amherst Mystery. By September 25, little more than a month and a half after he had said goodbye to Esther, a copy of *The Haunted House: A True Ghost Story* had reached the editorial offices of the *Chignecto Post*. Curiously, the newspaper that had expressed a keen interest in all Esther's troubles was not impressed with Hubbell's book, stating, "we cordially recommend the public not to read it."

While Hubbell was continuing with his acting career and promoting his book, Esther was getting on with her own life. She stayed with the Van Amburghs for a short time, looking after their children and cleaning the house. Then, in the fall, she got a job as a servant working in the home of Arthur Davidson, a neighbour of the Van Amburghs and a clerk of the Cumberland County Court. Davidson and his wife, Mary, had two sons, three-year-old Clarence and one-year-old Richard. The Davidson family attended the Methodist church in Amherst, so they knew Daniel and Olive Teed as well as Esther. Thirty-five-year-old Arthur had been a merchant before taking over the position with the County Court, a posting he may have received through family connections, as his father-in-law, Richard Huestis, was a Clerk of the Peace for the County of Cumberland and a Justice of the Peace.

The Davidsons were pleased with the work Esther did for them. Arthur wrote years later that "a better girl we never had since." He also described her as "not good-looking" and "very ignorant with only a common education." Knowing her reputation, the Davidsons watched her closely—Arthur claimed that "she seemed to fly downstairs." Esther's time with the Davidson family was also not without its strange occurrences. One evening, she was setting the table for tea and Arthur was reading the paper. All at once he was hit on the back of the head with a fork. Noting that while some people might doubt the girl and her stories about spirits, Davidson remarked, "when a man gets a whack on the head, it then, with him at least, assumes a reality."

Other things happened as well. Once, Davidson was just coming into the barn when Esther was leaving the building, having finished milking the cow. Inside the barn, about twenty-five feet from the door, was a box where Davidson kept curry combs and brushes for the animals. Davidson heard a noise and looked down to see one of his curry combs "running along the floor about eight or ten feet behind her." The comb hit the door post and stopped. Davidson picked it up and threw it back into the storage box. Mary Davidson witnessed "ashes, tea-leaves, scrubbing brushes, soap and mop rags, and an old ham bone often flying around." Davidson explained that while these goings on "sometimes put them out in their work," they put up with it as, at the time, help was hard to find, "especially help like her." But soon, even the easy-going Davidsons had had enough.

On November 3, Mary told Arthur that she was missing some things. She had looked everywhere for the cotton and tweed fabric she planned to make into a dress. Also missing were two skirts, a pair of men's trousers, a bed sheet, four pillow cases, some silver cutlery, and a mirror. Mary said she had suspected Esther of stealing and had confronted the girl, who denied taking anything. Davidson himself then questioned her. Esther told the Davidsons that the spirits, Bob and Maggie, were obviously up to their old tricks again. This time, however, her story was not believed. Davidson bluntly told Esther that he was going to the authorities, and the next day, November 4, he did just that, reporting the theft to the Amherst police and pointing the finger at his servant. A warrant was issued to search the premises of John Van Amburgh for the Davidsons' property. During this search, Bob the spirit struck again.

The November 6 edition of the *Chignecto Post* reported that on the morning of November 4, two barns had been destroyed by fire. One belonged to lawyer William T. Pipes. The other was Arthur Davidson's. The hay stored in Davidson's barn caught fire and it looked as though it had been started deliberately. Fortunately, thanks to a snow storm that morning, the fires did not spread to any other buildings.

While the Pipes and Davidson barns were alight, a search of the Van Amburghs' house yielded a number of the missing items. The *Chignecto Post* told its readers that "Esther's complicity in the theft and the mystery of the origin of the fire seemed to require a full investigation." The next day, when Esther and John Van Amburgh stood before the County Court of Nova Scotia at the Amherst courthouse, there were two magistrates on the bench: Justices William Cutten and James

Bliss, Daniel Teed's landlord. Both Esther and Van Amburgh were held in jail overnight and their examinations resumed the next day.

By then the police had all of Davidson's missing articles in their possession and brought them into the courtroom as evidence. The rest of the items had been obtained from Mrs. Van Amburgh, who told the searching constables that Esther had visited their farm Sunday afternoon and asked her husband to stop by the Davidsons the following evening and pick up a parcel. He did as he was asked, taking the incriminating bundle home with him. Neither Esther nor Van Amburgh had a defence attorney. At the conclusion of the examinations, Van Amburgh was free to go, but Esther was committed to trial for stealing and setting the two barns on fire. At the trial she was found guilty of theft and sentenced to four months' imprisonment.

Old Court House, Amherst, after 1887 fire.

The Amherst jail was a wooden structure, built in 1831. It was adjacent to the courthouse at the corner of Victoria and Lawrence streets, in what was then called Courthouse Square. On January 12, 1881, less than two years after Esther stood before the magistrate, a *Chignecto Post* editorial reported on the "crying necessity" for a new courthouse, describing the current one as "antiquated, ill smelling and inconvenient." The jail was in even worse condition. Its cells measured twelve by fourteen feet, with nine-foot ceilings. While a number of men would have shared the same cell, Esther, likely the only woman incarcerated at the time, would have had her own cell. The jailer during Esther's stay was Mathius Acorn, who had various careers through his life, including that of farmer and constable. Acorn and his wife, Catharine, lived in a house located on Lawrence Street, near the jail. Catharine, in the tradition of a jailer's wife, cooked, did laundry, and maintained the day-to-day running of

Original location of Amherst jail, attached to the Customs Excise building.

the facility. It was she who would have been in charge of Esther's welfare during her stay.

In the nineteenth century, Cumberland County did not provide many resources for the housing of criminals or the poor, so conditions at the Amherst jail in 1879 would have been primitive at best. Each cell contained a mattress, some thin blankets, and not much else. Holes cut into the floors of the cells served as toilets. In mid-November, the building would have been cold, even freezing, and Esther would have had to keep moving, pacing back and forth, in order to maintain some kind of warmth. The jail contained two stoves, which would have been kept going constantly during the fall and winter months. Since they were not located in the cells, however, they would not have been of much comfort to the prisoners. Olive, Daniel, and Jennie may have brought Esther some comforts from home, such as extra blankets and clothes.

It appears that Esther was never found guilty of arson. Sentencing was delayed at the time of her court appearances and then dropped completely. The arson charge might have been dropped after she pled guilty to the theft of the Davidsons' property or it could have been dismissed for some other reason. Perhaps the Davidson and Pipes families felt she had learned her lesson. Perhaps the court was lenient because it knew what she had been through the past year. In any event, Esther spent only one month in the Amherst jail. By December 20 she was free. The *Amherst Sentinel* was not sympathetic, reporting that the mystery this time was "how she got out before the end of the term of imprisonment."

Walter Hubbell learned of Esther's incarceration in a letter from Jennie written on November 13, 1879.

> *You write to know where esther is I must tell you the sad tail she is in Jail she has been thair for a week and has to stay for four months oh Mr Hubbell it is hard for hir and mutch harder for me for I think that I do feel it more than she dose for I cannot hold my head up when I go out for I think that people is looking at me and thinking of hir but I must tell you what they put hir in for she was living at Mr. Davisons and she took some of the clothes and took them out of mr. vanembourges and said that thay had been taken and thay found some of them in hir care and the barn was set on fire and bunt down to the ground and two others and they think that shee doun it for spite for she was the last one in the barn so that is all that I can tell you about hir at present...don't mencon what I said aboute esther to anyone that would think hard of it.*

Hubbell lamented the barn burning as the work of Bob the demon spirit and that the "judge and jury did not believe in ghosts, and I was not there to explain." He credited "her previous good character and virtuous life, and the knowledge of so many as to the true nature of her trouble" for Esther's early release.

Esther's time in jail traditionally marks the end of the Mystery—at least, no news of it was reported by the press after December 1879. Hubbell's account of Esther ends there as well. But life did go on.

CHAPTER 5

Life Afterwards

The more I pressed her with questions, the more irritated she became, and finally her husband intervened, and said that for $100 he would consent to her telling me all necessary details.
~ Hereward Carrington, Paranormal Researcher,
American Society of Psychical Research

After her release from jail in December 1879, Esther Cox moved back with Olive and Daniel to 6 Princess Street. During her incarceration the spirits—Bob, Maggie, and the others—stopped haunting her and never appeared again. All the other manifestations ceased as well. No more objects moved mysteriously about, no more pillows flew. There were no more knockings and no more fires. Esther's midnight trances and swellings never returned, and there were no further scratches or pinpricks. Walter Hubbell's explanation was that "Bob, the demon-ghost was finally scared away from Esther, by the incantations and conjurations of an Indian medicine man or witch doctor" and "promised never to follow or molest her." But the ever-eager newspapers carried no reports of any such exorcism and there are no known corroborations with his story. Esther and the Teeds were just relieved to start the new year by getting back to normal after a trying fifteen months.

Soon after, however, on March 31, 1880, sorrow visited the Teed home when two-year-old George died of scarlet fever. Black crepe was hung on the front door and over the windows and mirrors at 6 Princess Street, and the little fellow was laid to rest in the Amherst Cemetery on Church Street.

Despite this heartbreak, life for the Teed family continued much as it had before Esther's troubles had garnered so much interest. Daniel's employer, Amherst Boot and Shoe, prospered, and in April 1880 it reported a busy spring for its sixty-three employees. Jennie continued her work at the tailor shop, while Olive stayed home with remaining son William. In July Nannary's theatre troupe (minus Walter Hubbell) was back in town performing *Neck and Neck* at the Music Hall, and White's Oyster Saloon continued its bustling business. Many people forgot about Esther Cox and her ghosts. But not everyone: the faithful Rev. Dr. Clay continued his lectures on the Mystery. In October 1880 he presented the "Amherst Mystery" on three consecutive evenings at Hopewell Corners in Albert County, New Brunswick.

And the newspapers had not entirely forgotten Esther either. Their lasting impression of her resulting from the time when she held their almost undivided attention seems to be an unfavourable one. In fact, she became a figure of fun and ridicule. On August 11, 1881, almost three years after the beginning of her troubles, the *Chignecto Post* reported:

> A large crowd gathered in and about Justice Cutten's office on Thursday last, evidently on some exciting and all engrossing business. It was finally developed that the celebrated Esther Cox was a magnet and the performance was not altogether of a spiritual

character. Esther figured as a witness on behalf of Her Majesty the Queen, in a quasi criminal suit. Two lawyers were employed on either side and the whole affair was voted better than a menagerie.

Apparently the twenty-one-year-old Esther had been called as a witness against someone who had committed a minor offence, and her presence was cause for a lively gathering at the judge's office.

Less than six months later she became a married woman. On March 3, 1882, Esther wed Adam Porter, a thirty-six-year-old widower living in nearby Springhill. Originally from Middle River in Pictou County, Nova Scotia, Adam—the eighth of ten siblings and the youngest son of James and Jane Porter—moved to Springhill to work in its rapidly expanding coal-mining industry.

Springhill is thirty-three kilometres southeast of Amherst, on the northwestern edge of the Cobequid Hills, midway between the Minas Basin and the Northumberland Strait. Its original settlers, the Boss and Herrett families, were United Empire Loyalists who had served with the King's army in Harper's Ferry, Virginia, and claimed their service grants in Nova Scotia in 1790. Forty-three years later, in 1833, coal was discovered in the Springhill area on the property of Lodwick Hunter and private coal mining began. It would be another four decades, however, before the area's vast coal deposits began to be extracted on a large scale.

Until 1870, Springhill was a tiny community of fewer than two dozen people and five houses. For years attempts to establish a coal-mining industry there had failed, but then the Spring Hill Mining Company was formed and three years later the first carload of coal left Springhill by rail. Soon, two rival coal companies were working the mines until they merged in 1884 to form the Cumberland Railway and Coal Company. Men poured in from the coal-mining areas of Pictou County, Cape Breton, and even Britain, and by 1881 Springhill's population had expanded to nine hundred.

Esther herself may have relocated to this busy mining community to find work, as her family had done years before when they left Stewiacke for Amherst. A move from Amherst would also allow her to start a new life surrounded by people who were not so familiar with her and her story. If Esther was employed in Springhill before marrying Adam Porter, she would have been cleaning house, doing laundry, and looking after children. Domestic work was all she knew.

After their wedding, Esther and Adam settled down in one of the many workers' houses that had been built in the early 1870s by the Cumberland County Coal Company. The wood-framed, two-storeyed salt boxes, each accommodating two families, were built in rows of ten along Queen Street and Spruce Street—indeed, the area was known as "the rows" and its occupants were dubbed "rowsers." All new families who came to town for the mines moved into the rows and paid $3.00 a month rent. However humble, in such a house Esther finally became mistress of her own space and could manage it as she saw fit.

Esther maintained contact with her family in Amherst, telling them of the birth of her and Adam's son, James, in 1883 (their only child), and keeping up on the news of the growing Teed family. After the death of their son George, the Teeds went on to have six more children, all girls. Since Olive was often pregnant during the 1880s, she, Esther, and sister Nellie could commiserate on the trials and tribulations of raising children.

Esther also frequently received news from Colchester County and was saddened to hear of the deaths of the two people who had raised her. Her grandparents, Eleazar and Olive Dickey, after a long life together, died within two weeks of each other, Eleazar on April 3, 1888, and Olive eleven days later, on April 14.

In 1890, when Esther and Adam had been married for eight years and son James was seven, Mother Coo, a Pictou County fortune teller, predicted that Springhill would suffer a mining disaster in May of the following year. Since she had correctly foreseen two earlier Nova Scotia coal mine disasters, one at Westville's Drummond Mine in 1873, which claimed fifty-nine lives, and the other at Stellarton's Foord Pit in 1880, which killed fifty men, Mother Coo was taken seriously by the powers that be in Springhill. Early in 1891 a committee of inspectors reported the mines to be in excellent condition and probably among the safest in the province. But Mother Coo, although a few months off, would prove correct once more.

On Saturday, February 21, the day after the visit by a government inspector, a cold rain fell from a steel grey sky onto the town of Springhill. It was 12:43 p.m. and the miners had finished their half-hour dinner break. Just then Thomas Wilson, at the 1,900 level of Number One Mine, set off a dynamite charge to blast coal out of a seam. A crack in the material packed around the explosives allowed fire to escape into the air, igniting coal dust. The instantaneous explosion shot flames through Number One Mine and into Number Two through a connecting tunnel at the 1,300 level. Devastation followed leaving 125 men and boys killed, most outright; 4 others died later on. Barely a home in Springhill was left untouched by what became Canada's most devastating mining disaster of the nineteenth century. Relief efforts saw contributions come from across the country and the British Empire. Queen Victoria herself made a personal donation to the community.

Although the mines brought heartache and worry, they also caused Springhill to grow and prosper and by the 1890s it had a population of nearly five thousand. In 1893 Springhill became one of the first communities in the province to have electricity installed. On November 21, 1895, the first issue of the *Springhill Advertiser* rolled off the presses, calling itself "fearless, Independent and for the People."

Adam Porter died sometime before 1896 but neither the date nor the cause is known. As a coal miner's widow, Esther would have received financial support from the Employees Relief Fund, established in 1884 by the Cumberland Railway and Coal Company "to provide relief to employees and their families in the case of sickness, accident and death," but she would have had to go back to her former employment as a servant or take in laundry to make ends meet. Then, on July 23, 1896, thirty-six-year-old Esther (Cox) Porter married forty-four-year-old Peter Shannahan.

Newfoundland-born Peter Shannahan worked in the Springhill mines alongside Adam Porter. Like Adam, Peter had been living in Pictou County and came to Springhill when the mines opened up. Indeed, he, his wife Mary, and toddlers John and Margaret were among the first wave of economic migrants to the town. As early as 1873 Peter was working in the mines there, boring holes for the west engine foundation in the Number Two Mine and digging coal. By March 1875, however, he had become a widower, Mary having died at the age of twenty-nine. Left with two small children, Peter did not wait long to remarry. He and second wife, Eleanor Nash, were wed in the nearby community of Nappan on November 15, 1875.

By 1881 Peter and Eleanor were living in Maccan, another small village not far from Springhill. His sixty-seven-year-old widowed mother, Margaret, and his brother Thomas and wife, Bridget, lived nearby. Peter and Eleanor had seven daughters, but this second marriage was not to last long either. By 1891, Peter was a widower once more and living in Springhill with his children. His son John, now twenty-five, also worked in the mines while daughter Margaret ran the Shannahan household. After the deadly explosion of February 1891, Peter was among the first volunteers to go down into the mine, restoring ventilation and setting up temporary roof supports. Five years later, when Peter married for the third time, Esther took over the management of his family, adding thirteen-year-old James to the mix. The Shannahans were staunch Roman Catholics and leaders of the church in Springhill. Esther became a member of the Catholic Church upon her marriage to Peter.

Shortly after their wedding, Esther and Peter moved away from Springhill, likely in the search for better, more stable employment. Peter suffered from rheumatism, and the harsh conditions of Springhill's coal mines may have been too much for him. Esther, Peter, and their children became part of a huge flow of Maritimers during the late nineteenth and early twentieth centuries to the manufacturing towns along the eastern seaboard of the United States. The Shannahans immigrated to Brockton, Massachusetts, America's leading manufacturer and exporter of shoes. Indeed, since 1880, the town had been known as Shoe City. On their way through Maine, the Shannahans may have stopped to visit Esther's father, Archibald Cox, and his wife, Ann, who had been living in East Machias since the 1870s.

Brockton, thirty-one kilometres south of Boston, lies along the Salisbury Plain River. Although founded as long ago as

1645, the town became prominent only with the coming of the Industrial Revolution. In 1811 Micah Faxon travelled to Boston's Long Wharf to sell his homemade shoes, and later opened a shoe factory in Brockton, then called North Bridgewater. Faxon became a millionaire and his example inspired the small shoe factories that soon sprung up all over the town. The Civil War and technological advances turned the town into the world's leading shoe centre. Curiously, in 1874, when North Bridgewater's citizens voted on a new name for their town, they took the suggestion of a local businessman who had recently visited Ontario, perhaps not realizing they were honouring Sir Isaac Brock, a British hero of the War of 1812.

In its heyday, Brockton was a thriving modern town. Thomas Edison used it as the experimental site for many of his projects. It was the first community in the United States to place its electric wires underground, the first in the world to have its theatre lit by electricity, and the second in the world to use

Bird's eye view of Brockton, Massachusetts, circa 1908.

incandescent and arc lamps for lighting. By 1900 ninety-nine of Brockton's factories made shoes and shoe-related products and exported them to Cuba, the United Kingdom, Italy, Denmark, Belgium, France, and Mexico.

When Esther and Peter Shannahan arrived in Brockton, its population was rapidly approaching forty thousand. The city was inundated by Irish, French-Canadian, Swedish, Italian, Polish, and Portuguese immigrants all searching for work. It was a much bigger, noisier, prosperous, and diverse community than the couple had ever experienced. Esther, if she desired, could shop at Polish bakeries and Syrian grocery stores.

While Peter started work as a labourer with Brockton's new sewer department, Esther had a large household to look after. Though Peter's oldest children, John and Margaret, remained behind in Springhill, each to marry and raise a family, his five remaining daughters (two having died) had moved to Brockton with their father, new stepmother, and thirteen-year-old stepbrother, James. Teenagers Sarah and Eleanor, and Mary, Annie, and Teresa, in their early twenties, were all old enough to help around the house and to look for employment as housekeepers, nannies, and office or factory workers. Eventually, sixteen-year-old James found work as a finisher in a shoe factory. And to their already large blended family, Esther and Peter, after a stillbirth, added two more sons: Peter Andrew, born in February 1899 and Albert, their last child, born in 1902—who was struck down by scarlet fever on February 22, 1907.

By the end of the first decade of the twentieth century, 90 percent of the homes in Brockton were owned by men working in shoe factories. Esther and Peter were never so fortunate as to own their own home, however, and their life in Shoe City seems to have been one of economic struggle. Peter's rheumatism worsened over the years, and after 1902 he no longer worked full time. James's employment at the shoe factory was often part time as well, and by 1906 he was a married man, and gone off to live with his new wife, Nellie. So Esther, almost from the beginning of their life in Brockton, was the principal breadwinner of the Shannahan family.

She made money as a self-employed laundress, taking other people's soiled clothing, bedding, and curtains into her home. The City of Brockton was one of her clients, and she was described by one department as "very hard-working, respectable, honest and reliable." Doing laundry before electricity was in common use was both a craft and arduous labour. From start to finish, one load of laundry could take days to complete and the disruption, caused by baskets of dirty clothes, lines full of damp bedding, and mountains of ironing, was the reason that those who could afford to sent their laundry out. The work required a lot of upper-body strength for the lifting, carrying, and wringing out of heavy items. Water, if a home lacked indoor plumbing, would be transported from an outdoor well or pump. It would then need to be heated to wash the clothes, while more would be required later on for rinsing. Everything would then need to be hung outside to dry. On rainy days laundry was hung around the house. Then the ironing commenced.

Soiled laundry would be delivered to the Shannahan home throughout the week, so there were likely always dirty clothes around. It would have been crowded and hot, and Esther would have solicited any of the girls remaining at home to help her to sort the laundry and keep Peter Andrew and Albert amused and away from underfoot.

Despite the many difficulties it presented, taking in laundry also had its positive aspects for Esther. It allowed her to work from her home, obviating the need to hire a babysitter to look after her little boys, while providing her an income of about five dollars a week. It was something, but it was not enough.

From 1905 to 1912 Peter Shannahan's name appears regularly in the City of Brockton's Poor Rolls. During this time he and Esther received money to buy fuel three to four times a month, in addition to cash for groceries, shoes, milk, and medical attention. They lived in Brockton's downtown core, among the workers' houses and factories, and moved many times, an indication of an inability to keep up rent payments or of a constant search for less expensive accommodations.

It was around the time little Albert fell ill with scarlet fever that Hereward Carrington, a paranormal researcher with the American Society of Psychical Research in New York, paid a call to the Shannahans at their 14 East Union Street home. On January 26 and 27, 1907, Carrington, on his way back from an investigation of paranormal activity in Windsor, Nova Scotia, had stopped in Amherst hoping for an update on the Mystery. He had knocked on the door of 6 Princess Street, then rented by Mrs. Rebecca Cahill who assured Carrington that she and her family had experienced no trouble with spirits since living there. He had also visited Daniel and Olive Teed now living on Douglas Avenue. Olive gave him Esther's current address in Brockton, telling him that she had not seen her sister for many years.

When Carrington got to Brockton, he found Esther and Peter in an unhappy state. He described their home as a cottage and their living conditions as "squalid." Esther did not want to talk about her long-ago exploits, saying she was "afraid that they might come back," and was reluctant to tell her story. Carrington seems to have been quite persistent with her and gave up only when Peter said that he would allow Esther to tell her story for one hundred dollars. The researcher took great offence to this proposal, stating that, "I should in that case have no guarantee whatever that I was not furnished with a hundred dollars worth of lies—as bought testimony—particularly in the case of this character." He promptly put on his hat and left the premises, "none too pleased with the interview, or the late medium and her husband." With a sick child on their hands, and their ongoing financial problems, the Shannahans would have had little patience with a stranger suddenly appearing with questions about Esther's past. And they could have certainly used any money that Carrington might have offered for her story.

Five years later, in the fall of 1912, Esther fell seriously ill herself, and died suddenly on November 8 in her home on Crescent Avenue, at the age of fifty-two. E. G. McSweeney, her attending physician, identified the cause of death as acute gastritis. An irritation or inflammation of the lining of the stomach sometimes referred to as dyspepsia, gastritis can be brought on by a number of factors including infection, auto-immune disease, tuberculosis, or excessive use of alcohol or aspirin. Patients with severe gastritis can experience stomach bleeding, sweating, a rapid heart beat, breathing problems, and pain in the chest or stomach. In the days leading up to her death, Esther would have experienced a loss of appetite. Interestingly, while her death certificate cites gastritis as the cause of death, the *Brockton Times,* perhaps using information supplied by the family, identified it as heart disease, which could also entail a range of causes and symptoms.

Whatever had happened, Esther was gone, leaving behind a husband, two sons, and many step-children. The *Brockton Times* describes her as a well-known resident of the city. She had been heavily involved with the parish affairs of her church, St. Colman of Cloyne's, where her funeral was held on November 10.

Father J. J. Dermody performed a high mass of requiem for the repost of her soul. Esther's casket was covered with floral tributes from her family, including a mound of white chrysanthemums from Peter and a standing crescent and cross from friends in the finishing room of James's employer, the J. M. O'Donnell shoe factory. Esther was laid to rest in section 35, bordering North Cary Street, in Brockton's Calvary Cemetery. With her death, her side of the story of the Great Amherst Mystery was lost forever. Today, Esther's direct descendants and those of her sons, James and Peter Andrew, live throughout the United States, while descendants of her sister Nellie Snowden, including great-grandniece Tammy Smith, reside in the Amherst area.

After Esther's death, Peter moved into the 417 Crescent Street home of his daughter Sarah and her husband, James Stack, a worker with the water commission. Less than two years later, on March 13, 1914, the *Brockton Times* announced "Find Shannahan Dead in Bed." At 7:30 A.M. that morning, the Stacks' seven-year-old daughter Eleanor ran downstairs to tell her mother she smelled gas outside her grandfather's bedroom. Sarah opened the door to find her father lying in bed with the gas jets on and the windows closed. Sarah quickly turned off the jets and opened the window, but it was too late. Peter Shannahan was dead at the age of sixty-two. The medical examiner pronounced cause of death as the inhaling of illuminating gas. The *Times* went on to say that "on the evening before his death Peter was in good spirits, joking and laughing with the members of the family, as was his custom. It was believed that during the night he got up and lighted the gas and going back to bed again did not turn them off." Peter's family adamantly declared to the press that Peter's death was wholly accidental. Sarah told reporters that as well as rheumatism, which kept him indoors much of the time, her father also suffered from a heart condition. Yet, he was described as "not despondent" and as "looking forward to the advent of good weather when he could sit outside on the porch." The news item did note that he had "brooded over his wife's death of the last two years." He was buried alongside Esther at the Calvary Cemetery.

Olive Teed lived for many years after the death of her younger sister—indeed, she survived many of her own children. Ethel Louisa Teed, born about 1885, was the oldest of Daniel's and Olive's many daughters. She succumbed to a brain tumour at the age of thirty-three but as young as she was she outlived most of her sisters. Teresa, born in 1890, lived only six months, while Ida died at age six that same year. Jennie, born in 1895, lived to be just thirteen. Two other daughters, Mabel, born about 1888, and Myrtle, born in 1893, may have lived to adulthood but their death and burial records have not been found.

Gravestone for Esther (Cox) Shannahan, Peter Shannahan, and their son Albert in Brockton, Massachusetts.

Daniel and Olive celebrated the births and mourned the deaths of their daughters in their own home on Douglas Avenue, which they bought in 1884. Both lived into old age and they were married for sixty years. Daniel passed away in 1934 at the age of eighty-five, while Olive lived on for another nine years, dying in 1943 at the age of ninety-three. A family source suggests that, in later years, the Teeds moved to Baltimore, Maryland, where they died and are buried, but their burial records have not been

Teed family gravestone in the Amherst Cemetery.

found. Their young daughters, along with son George, are buried in the Amherst Cemetery. William, their oldest child, lived to age sixty-two, dying in Pictou on May 10, 1937. Jennie Cox moved from Amherst to the United States and married, but beyond that, her life remains an unknown. Whatever knowledge she had of the Great Amherst Mystery has been lost to history as well.

Walter Hubbell, the chronicler of Esther's exploits, also outlived his subject by many years. Throughout his life he continued his interest in spiritualism, attending seances and lectures on the subject. His penchant for unusual characters seems to have continued as well. On December 14, 1887, a New York City newspaper reported that,

> Walter Hubbell was excited yesterday morning at police headquarters when he reported that his friend, Edward Serviss, had been kidnapped in broad daylight by two men who said that they wanted him for a crime committed in Chicago. Mr. Hubbell was surprised to learn that his friend was one of the most notorious swindlers of the West, and that he was on his way to Omaha to answer a charge of forgery on a requisition of the Governor of Nebraska.

In May 1889 Hubbell was called to a New York City coroner's office to provide evidence of what he had witnessed the night of May 12 at the prestigious Lamb's Club, a private gathering place for entertainment industry professionals at 70 West 36th Street. On that particular evening, he had attended a performance by the young mentalist Washington Irving Bishop. While attempting to read someone's mind, Bishop had collapsed twice.

The second time he did not regain consciousness. His body was taken to the city morgue where an autopsy was performed. In the middle of the operation, Bishop's mother and wife stormed into the room proclaiming that he was a victim of catalepsy, a physical condition usually associated with catatonic schizophrenia and characterized by muscular rigidity and a trance-like state. They were certain that Bishop had not died at the Lamb's Club. They claimed that he frequently went into such trances when performing, and that it was the hasty autopsy that had, in fact, killed him. An investigation ensued and all in attendance on that fateful night were called to testify. Days later Hubbell was one of the pallbearers at Bishop's funeral.

In addition to his interest in spiritualism and the world beyond, Hubbell was a writer and poet. Besides a family history, in 1886 he published *Marcus Brutus and Other Verse*. And although a lifelong bachelor, in 1888 he provided his thoughts on wedlock in *The Curse of Marriage: A True Story of Domestic Life*. Hubbell maintained a number of memberships in organizations that reflected his interests: the Fairfield County Historical Society, the New York Genealogical and Biographical Society for Physical Research, and the Actors' Order of Friendship.

During the 1890s he appeared in several Shakespearean productions: *Macbeth*, *Hamlet*, *Othello*, and *Richard III*. In 1905, under the management of Gordon and Bennett, he began a role as Aguila in *A Royal Slave*. It was this production that brought him back to Amherst in May 1908, appearing at the Academy of Music. After finishing his Maritime tour in Yarmouth, Nova Scotia, Hubbell travelled back to Amherst by ferry and train, arriving on June 2. A year after researcher Hereward Carrington had come to town with questions about Esther Cox, Hubbell was back on his old stomping grounds with his own inquiries.

He stayed in Amherst for three weeks, boarding once again at 6 Princess Street, this time with Rebecca Cahill. Hubbell renewed his acquaintance with Daniel and Olive and contacted other individuals he had known there almost three decades earlier. He wanted to catch up with Esther's story and visit his old friends. But this was not just a pleasure trip. Hubbell was eager to update his book, *The Haunted House*, now entitled *The Great Amherst Mystery*, which had sold well over the intervening years. His main objective was to secure proof against dissenters that the manifestations he had recorded in his first edition were indeed true. He secured what he called a testamentary document on June 10, 1908. It was signed by sixteen witnesses, including Daniel and Olive, J. Albert Black, the former editor of the *Chignecto Post*, and Charles Tupper Hillson, the current landlord of 6 Princess Street. Included in all subsequent editions of his book, the document states in part:

> *Having of our own personal knowledge and not by or through hearsay or belief, absolutely known, seen and heard individually all or some of the demonstrations, manifestations, and communications of an invisible, intelligent and malicious power within the atmosphere that continued its awe-inspiring and mysterious operations in the home of Daniel Teed....and elsewhere in the actual presence of his sister-in-law Esther Cox...as narrated by Walter Hubbell...in a book... entitled The Great Amherst Mystery.*

Hubbell's book on Esther Cox and the Great Amherst Mystery has never been out of print and has been periodically republished with a new foreword or introduction.

Walter Hubbell as "Aguila" in *A Royal Slave*, circa 1908.

In 1887, the Hubbell family had moved from Philadelphia to New York City, and Walter Hubbell lived in that city for the rest of his life, residing with his mother and then his siblings until his death, in Queens, on January 25, 1932, at the age of eighty-one. He never publicly wavered in his belief that Esther Cox had been haunted by evil spirits.

The Teeds' former home continued to be inhabited for many years after Esther and then Daniel and Olive had left it behind. Landlord and magistrate James Bliss lived there for a number of years, then sold it in 1885 to George Hewson of Oxford. Sometime after 1908, the house itself was moved to Davidson Street, away from the business district and into a residential neighbourhood, where, of course, it assumed a new street number. The infamous "haunted house" no longer stands. It was torn down sometime during the early twentieth century. Its Princess Street location was occupied for many years by a Canadian Tire outlet. Today offices for Nova Scotia Community Services are located where Esther and the Teed family once lived.

And what became of Bob MacNeill, Esther's beau and perhaps the catalyst for the Great Amherst Mystery? Quitting Amherst after that last buggy ride with Esther, he was never heard of again according to subsequent articles and books. But Bob's whereabouts were indeed known, by most of Cumberland County, and most importantly, by the Teed family and by Esther herself.

On January 30, 1879, five months after the infamous buggy ride, the *Saint John Daily Telegraph* informed its readers that Bob MacNeill had spent time in Fairville, a small but busy community on the outskirts of Saint John, New Brunswick. During the 1870s businesses in Fairville included blacksmith shops, furniture dealers, saw mills, and boot and shoe makers. Bob needed a job and likely went to New Brunswick to find work. He did not, however, stay there for long: the *Telegraph* article also mentioned that Bob was "now in Malagash." So, during much of the time that the Great Amherst Mystery was in full swing and the object of intense scrutiny by both the public and the press, Bob MacNeill was in Cumberland County, just seventy kilometres from Amherst, working on the family farm. Indeed, despite his parents' concerns about his physical abilities, Bob ended up with their farm after all. The brothers who owned the property both decided to move away and each gave Bob his share in return for his caring for Susan, their widowed mother. He spent the rest of his life there, raising cattle and milking cows, tending vegetable gardens and making shoes. Bob was a hard worker with a strong personality. He held definite opinions on politics, religion, and any number of subjects, and did not hesitate to air them. He was a force, not always a popular one, to be reckoned with in the Malagash area.

One elderly member of the community remembered Bob MacNeill as a person who "could cause things to happen." Once, Bob went to Israel Langille's farm to speak to someone working there. Men were gathered in the threshing room and the place was noisy. The person whom Bob approached told him that he was too busy and could not see him at the moment. The story goes that "all at once he caused everything to stop and the belts all flew off." "Now," Bob said, "you will talk to me."

There was a relative of Bob's who lived in Malagash, a man with the last name of Teed, whom Bob seemed to take particular delight in goading and tormenting. Mr. Teed was a road hog who drove his horse and buggy in the middle of the road, crowding everyone else out of the way. Bob was getting tired of moving to the side of the road whenever he met Teed, so one day, as the old gentleman once again started to crowd him over towards the ditch, Bob lost his temper. He picked up his crutch and swung it at the older man. Maybe he hit him, maybe not. In any case Teed took Bob to court, where he was found guilty of assault and fined. Weeks later Bob got his revenge. The next time he met his nemesis on the road, Bob was accompanied by another man whom he warned in advance, "You see nothing." Bob then promptly steered his wagon directly towards Teed's buggy, running the old gentleman completely off the road and into the ditch.

Bob's temper and outspokenness earned him at least two nicknames in the Malagash area. Some people called him "Burkus," the meaning of which is not clear. Others called him "Devil," the meaning of which is all too clear. Bob did not care what others thought about him and he did little to discourage their bad opinion. One summer's day he was at Malagash Point mowing hay when a section of the forest between the hay field and the MacNeill farm caught fire. The main road was filled with thick, black smoke. At the end of the work day Bob decided that, instead of taking the long way around to avoid the fire, he would travel his regular route home even if it meant going directly through the smoke. Those who saw Bob emerging through the black billows with his horse and wagon were not really surprised. Who else but the Burkus, the Devil, could have survived that?

Bob's mother, Susan MacNeill, outlived her husband, Samuel, by thirty-one years. As she got older and began to decline, Bob became increasingly concerned about her. Susan's bedroom was located on the main floor of the house, just off the kitchen. Bob would sleep there with a cot positioned lengthwise across the door of her room so he would be alerted if she attempted to leave the house during the night. As Susan grew increasingly feeble, Bob hired a young woman from the community, Louisa Ann Ralph, to live with them, do the housework, and look after his mother. Susan MacNeill died on June 29, 1904. Soon after, Bob and Louisa, despite an age difference of thirty-three years, began a relationship and married. On August 23, 1905, seventeen-year-old Louisa gave birth to their only child, Robert Nelson. Bob and Louisa lived together for fifteen years, until he died of tuberculosis on October 10, 1919. Louisa remarried and continued to live in the area until her death in October 1975. Nelson MacNeill grew up and married. Today, his three sons, Kenley, Eldon, and Ian, live in Nova Scotia.

Eldon MacNeill tells a family story that provides Bob's explanation for why he had to leave Amherst so abruptly. "There was a woman there charged with witchcraft and one of the reasons he left was that they were going to make him go to court and testify against her. So he got out of the county. This woman was capable of starting fires right there in the middle of the table."

While we will never know Bob's side of the story concerning his relationship with Esther, this tidbit he left behind does provide some clues as to how he viewed the situation and to his personality. He needed to provide his family with a good reason for leaving Amherst, a place where he had been established for a number of years and where he had a steady job. To describe Esther as a witch, capable of doing him harm if he spoke against her, is evidence that he believed a story of the supernatural would be accepted on his return home. It also shows his talent for telling tall tales and for exaggeration, talents he may have used on Esther when they were courting.

But Bob McNeill was not the only one with opinions and explanations about Esther Cox and the Great Amherst Mystery.

Bob MacNeill, his wife Louisa (Ralph) MacNeill, and their son Robert Nelson, circa 1908.

CHAPTER 6

What They Thought It Was

> *A hundred and fifty-years ago Esther Cox would have been drowned as a witch. Those were the days of superstition. Today no one will have the temerity to suggest that there is any element of the supernatural in her case. These are times of special wisdom. And yet here is a rebuke to the whole great economy of modern philosophy, that the phenomena of an uneducated, unsophisticated rural life defies explanation. Are we so very wise after all?*
> ~ THE WESLEYAN, MAY 31, 1879

Attempts to explain the Great Amherst Mystery began soon after Esther's plight became common knowledge, and they continued into the twentieth century. Along with the explanations came the labelling of Esther. Bob MacNeill called her a witch, a label applied to many a misunderstood woman down through the centuries. Other, more worldly men like J. Albert Black and Dr. Aaron Alward thought she was a medium, capable of communicating with the dead. Dr. Thomas Carritte and the Rev. Robert Temple believed her to be a battery or magnet, a conductor of electricity. Esther herself said she was under the spell of mesmerism. Walter Hubbell considered her a victim of evil spirits, and in the twentieth century one researcher of psychical phenomena concluded that she suffered from what he called a "dual personality." The newspapers reported on it all, in the interest of public information and, more importantly, to sell papers. There were many possibilities, it seems, when it came to the young woman the *Wesleyan* described as rural, uneducated, and unsophisticated.

The belief that Esther was a medium, a go-between for the living and the spirit world, sprang from a knowledge of and interest in spiritualism, considered both a religion and a science, which was extremely popular during the latter half of the nineteenth century in the United States. Following the death and devastation brought on by the Civil War (1861–65), thousands turned to spiritualism when traditional religions could not relieve their pain or provide them with reassuring answers about the fate of their lost loved ones. Spiritualism guaranteed life after death, and, like the Great Amherst Mystery, it too evolved from humble beginnings.

In 1847 John and Margaret Fox left their family farm near Belleville, Ontario, and relocated to Hydesville, a village in upstate New York. Their older children, Leah and David, were sent to nearby Rochester while the two youngest, fourteen-year-old Maggie and eleven-year-old Katie, joined their parents in a small cottage that the local community said was haunted. One night, during the late winter of 1848, the family, after retiring, heard noises that sounded like knockings on the ceiling and walls and the movement of furniture. They assumed these disturbances were caused by the ghost that haunted the place. Many believers consider the date of March 31, 1848, when a "spirit" responded to young Katie's request to repeat the sound she made when snapping her fingers, to be the birthday of spiritualism. It was at that moment that the veil separating the living and the dead was lifted and communication between the two worlds was established. Mrs. Fox immediately ran to tell the neighbours.

The Fox sisters began regular conversations with the spirit, believed to be that of a peddler murdered in the house years before. They "spoke" to him by a system of knocks: one meaning yes, two meaning no. They also devised a code for distinguishing the letters of the alphabet so that words could be spelled out. Neighbours swarmed to the Fox home with questions of their own that they wanted the spirit, with the aid of Katie and Maggie, to answer. The Fox sisters also had their sceptics who bombarded the house, accosting the family with accusations of fraud whenever they left the premises. In order to escape the fracas, Katie and Maggie were sent away to join their siblings in Rochester where they continued their demonstrations.

Soon after moving to Rochester, the two girls were introduced to a family of Quakers interested in their ability to speak to the dead. The Quakers, in turn, introduced them to their larger religious community and to others disenchanted with traditional religion and its unwillingness to take a stand against problems such as slavery, women's rights, and alcohol. Through the Quakers, and with older sister Leah as their manager, Maggie and Katie found their way to New York, where from the 1850s to the late 1880s they were celebrated mediums, performing seances to large public audiences and select private gatherings. They were the toast of the town and soon became wealthy.

The practice of conversing with the dead was named spiritualism, and it quickly attracted thousands of followers, many from the upper classes. Hundreds of people, other than the Fox sisters, suddenly became aware of their own ability to communicate with the spirit world. Throughout the United States spiritualism became a craze and a business, as well as a religion, attracting into its fold the famous and the revered, including James Fenimore Cooper, Sojourner Truth, and Mary Todd Lincoln, who was distraught over the deaths of her son William and husband, President Abraham Lincoln.

Just five years after the Fox household spirit had responded to Katie, newspapers were regularly reporting on similar spirit phenomena from around the country, and books and periodicals on the subject abounded. Along with the seances, itinerant speakers held lectures on spiritualism, mesmerism, and other "occult sciences." Beginning in the 1860s people could not only communicate with their departed loved ones, but also see them again when New York's William Mumler set up his shop as the best known of a number of so-called spirit photographers.

Spiritualism's mass appeal was by no means limited to the United States. Britain soon had its share of spiritualist mediums and followers. Queen Victoria, devastated by the death of her beloved Albert, is said to have been an adherent. Spiritualism soon spread into Canada as well. In 1854 writer Susanna Moodie became a follower after meeting Katie Fox in Belleville. It was soon a topic of discussion throughout the country, with the requisite seances and lectures held in homes and lecture halls. In July 1875 two prominent American spiritualists were invited to speak to Toronto's secularist Liberal Club.

The appeal of spiritualism was manifold. It was considered capable of accomplishing what traditional religion and science could not: solving the mystery of life after death and bringing instant gratification and comfort to those who had lost loved ones. Now, through a medium, the living and their deceased friends and family members could keep in touch, the living questioning the dead about the hereafter. No longer was there any reason to fear death, for it was evident that life went on.

Spiritualism, while popular with both sexes, held a particular appeal for women, many of whom found their "voice" within its fold. Spiritualism was "discovered" by a woman, and women, perceived as having more pliant and receptive natures than men, were regarded as ideal conduits for communication between the living and the dead. Starting with the Fox sisters, many female mediums took centre stage, around the seance table and on lecture platforms, to receive and transmit messages from the spirit world.

By 1878, when Esther Cox's manifestations began, belief in spiritualism was on the wane in North America, its supporters under attack by non-believers and its practitioners subject to constant scrutiny and to tests of their ability and credibility. But it was by no means dead. During the first thirty years of its existence, spiritualism's practices became well known in Canada from the largest cities to the smallest communities. The residents of Amherst would have been aware of how it worked through books, newspapers, itinerant performers, and from their own travels.

On May 29, 1879, the *Chignecto Post* carried a story about a Boston medium currently performing in Saint John. It was J. Albert Black, the curious editor of the *Chignecto Post*, who taught Esther and the Teeds the commonly used knocking code for communication with the spirits. And the inhabitants of 6 Princess Street knew how to conduct seances. Indeed, the day Walter Hubbell met Esther he had been invited to take part in a seance. Although it was more likely that Esther learned how to conduct a seance from Black or from family or friends, she could also have read about it in one of the many how-to books and articles available on the subject. Readers were encouraged to form "spirit circles" in their own homes, whether a professional medium was present or not. The literature advised that one could never be sure when a natural-born medium would be discovered, and that there was usually at least one to be found in every household. Other tips included having an alternating male-female seating arrangement about a round table and not allowing individuals who disliked each other to participate in the same circle. Each session should begin with a prayer and a hymn. One person was to be chosen to address the spirits, then dim the lights and see what happened. If the spirits did not respond, the writers advised, use a different assortment of sitters. Access to the spirit world was assured regardless of age, creed, or social standing.

Individuals such as Esther, who were capable of moving objects, were considered to be powerful physical mediums. The seances Esther conducted in Saint John for Dr. Aaron Alward and his friends would have commenced with the men and their wives seated around a table and holding hands. Esther then would have taken command, calling upon the spirits that surrounded her, like Bob Nickle and Maggie Fisher, to come forward and answer the group's questions, and she would have been given the names of the departed to whom Dr. Alward and his group wished to speak. Esther stayed in Saint John for three weeks, leading seances and meeting people. Hubbell tells us that the Saint John group was satisfied with the results and "witnessed various phases of the power and talked with the ghost by the aid of knocks on the walls and household furniture. Other ghosts came and conversed also, by knocking."

Dr. Thomas Carritte was among the first to observe Esther's manifestations and the first to attempt to treat the swelling of her body and the trances she experienced. On several occasions he used varying mixtures and amounts of "a bromide of potassium, brandy, morphine and laudanum" to quiet what he referred to as her "nervous excitement." Despite his attentions to her, Dr. Carritte was not sure what was troubling Esther: in the November 7, 1878, *Chignecto Post*, he claimed to "have no theory whatsoever to offer." He was obviously thinking about what it might be, however, and in December 1878, during Esther's first days working at White's Oyster Saloon, he conducted a series of tests on her to ascertain if she was, as some believed, a magnet or a human battery, and as such, the source of an electrical current.

In the 1870s electricity was not yet a part of everyday life, and many still considered it a semi-magical force that defied the laws of nature. Most people did not understand how electricity was generated or transmitted and believed that it was possible for human bodies to manufacture it. Dr. Carritte reasoned that the knocking sounds and movement of objects were not caused by spirits but by an overabundance of electricity in Esther's body, which needed to be contained. He believed some sort of insulating material was required to block the flow of electricity and end the manifestations. He described his experiments to Dr. Edwin Clay in a letter dated December 17, 1878.

"I first stood her on a glass bottle and they [the knockings] ceased immediately, but would recommence the moment she step'd off the bottles, then had her bed put on insulators and it had the same effect, but she became very ill and tremendous nervous excitement ensued followed by a heavy mesmeric sleep, had to remove the insulators and let the electricity pass off. Knockings went on as usual." There were obviously those who disagreed with Dr. Carritte's and Dr. Clay's view of Esther's situation. Carritte's letter confided that "the opposition are acting entirely from hearsay and prejudice."

The Reverend Robert Temple was just as mystified as Dr. Carritte and he too expressed his puzzlement in the November 7 issue of the *Chignecto Post*: "I cannot give any solution of this mystery." Like Carritte, Temple saw Esther's troubles as emanating from the world of science, of which humans knew little. "I believe these phenomena to be worthy of scientific attention and investigations, as I have no doubt they are reconcilable with known laws. I have not come to regard them as supernatural, or as manifestations from the land of spirits. The meaningless character of the performances forbids any such conclusion. The age with all its discoveries has only reached the outskirts—the border land of the great work of electricity, of which these may only be phases." For Temple, the knocking on walls and the gyration of pillows was too commonplace to be the work of supernatural forces, and he believed that Carritte was on the right track with his experiments. Temple did advise Esther to pray and to sleep with a small bible under her pillow. And he was not the only one who saw Scripture as a way to ease her distress.

During the summer of 1879 Daniel received a letter from a Mr. Alexander Hamilton, who advised him to have Esther write out chapter 2, verse 3 of the Book of Habakkuk upon small slips of paper. This passage deals with the prophet's troubling visions from which he asks God for relief. Habakkuk is instructed to write about the visions he sees. The passage reads, "for still the vision awaits its time; it hastens to the end—it will not lie. If it seem slow, wait for it; it will surely come, it will not delay." Hamilton directed the Teeds that, when Esther next left the house and all the spirits with her, they were to paste the slips of paper over the doors and windows. Upon returning, Esther would enter the house, but the spirits, reading the Scripture,

Letter to Dr. Edwin Clay from William Henry Rogers, Inspector of Fisheries for Nova Scotia, December 8, 1878.

would flee from the word of God and the girl would be free at last. It is not known whether the family tried this experiment.

The Rev. Edwin Clay, however, also saw the workings of science in Esther's plight. During his continuing lecture series on the Great Amherst Mystery in Nova Scotia and New Brunswick, he declared that Esther was a human battery, at the mercy of her physical powers. He also defended Esther in the pulpit against the criticisms of Dr. Nathan Tupper, who maintained she was either a mesmerist or a fraud. Interestingly, Esther agreed with Tupper that the powers of mesmerism were behind the Great Amherst Mystery.

While North America gave birth to spiritualism, its helpmate mesmerism originated in France some eighty years earlier. In the 1770s the German physician Franz Mesmer theorized that every living being, ghostly spirit, and inanimate object possessed a natural energy transferable from one to another. He called this transference animal magnetism. Dr. Mesmer believed that illness could be cured if a healthy individual knew how to channel their natural energy to the sick person. He began to experiment with this theory by gazing into his patients' eyes, touching them, or moving his hands around just slightly above the surface of their bodies. This practice came to be known as mesmerism.

Though Mesmer's results were mixed and controversial, the French upper class popularized the practice, and mesmerism soon spread to Britain, where Charles Dickens was a proponent. In the United States and Canada, it first appeared at country fairs where a "trained mesmerist" would gaze into people's eyes. After the development of hypnotism in the 1840s, hypnotic trances were soon added to the mesmerist's routine.

Although never considered quite as respectable as spiritualism, mesmerism did have its followers and practitioners. Mesmerists set up shop as healers, claiming they could cure sickness by manipulating the flow of electric energy, exchanging their positive energy for the negative energy of the patient. Mesmerism, like spiritualism, was regarded as a democratic power that could be learned and harnessed by practically anyone. Books explaining the history of animal magnetism and the secrets of mesmerism were available to an eager audience. Those who wanted to become healers required only a good spirit, mental concentration, and the ability to master a searching and piercing "magnetic gaze," which could be learned through practice and self-control. Despite its perceived ability to cure, mesmerism and its possibilities for controlling others could also be abused. Most mesmerists were men; many of their subjects were women.

It is in his interview with the *Chignecto Post* that Reverend Temple tells us that "Miss Cox herself imagines she is under the influence of a young man, who appears to have picked up some books on mesmerism and becoming versed in it, has been experimenting on her." It is easy to imagine Bob MacNeill's interest in mesmerism and the potential it held for having others submit to his will. He might have read about the phenomenon himself, it might have been a topic of discussion among friends or family, possibly even at 6 Princess Street, or he could have seen mesmerists perform somewhere in Cumberland County. In any case it is quite possible that he attempted to impress Esther with his abilities in that area at some time during their courtship, perhaps even on the night of the buggy ride, throwing her a magnetic gaze and proclaiming that she was now under his power.

Despite the *Wesleyan*'s claims that, by 1879, the world was too far advanced for anyone to admit that the supernatural played a role in Esther's troubles, Walter Hubbell was not afraid to venture in that direction. In fact, he saw the spirit world as the only solution to the Great Amherst Mystery. While Hubbell's supposed initial response to reading about Esther in the newspapers was to label her as a fraud to be exposed, he soon, whether due to the perceived earning potential or to naivety, came to regard her as a spiritual medium and a victim of evil forces. Despite his professed experience as an "investigator of the supermundane" with a keen nose for uncovering spiritual frauds, Hubbell was, in fact, an ardent believer in the supernatural and looked for evidence of the spirit world everywhere.

And while he regularly attended church services, not all his religious beliefs were traditional. He was interested in many of the new ideas about the nature of the world and the afterlife that were being tossed about in his time. He was aware of the new teaching of theosophy, a combination of numerous philosophies, founded in 1875. Adherents of theosophy believed that human beings possessed what they called astral bodies, which existed in tandem with physical bodies. After death the astral body left its physical packaging behind and lived on another plane that was separate from, but equal to, life on earth. Hubbell believed that under certain circumstances, like the presence or absence of human electricity—which he called "vital magnetism"—these two worlds opened up to each other and people living on earth could interact with residents of the astral plane, who would appear to them as ghosts. Hubbell believed that this is what happened to Esther Cox.

Hubbell reasoned that Bob MacNeill was as much a victim as Esther. He surmised that Bob's body generated a large amount of "vital magnetism," which attracted the astral body of the deceased, evil Bob Nickle to him. It was this evil astral body that made Bob do nasty things, such as, perhaps, whatever happened between him and Esther on the night of the buggy ride. According to Hubbell, Esther, in a panic that fateful night, "suffered the derangement of her entire system," which led to the depletion of her own human electricity. This made her system vulnerable to the evil ghost, who immediately left Bob MacNeill's body and settled into hers, causing the strange manifestations that became the Great Amherst Mystery.

Hubbell also concluded that after Esther had been "cured" by the Mi'kmaq medicine man, the evil astral body left her and, needing somewhere to go, returned to the body of Bob MacNeill. Hubbell claimed that during the time when Esther was the unwilling victim of the evil spirit of Bob Nickle, Bob MacNeill had "led an uneventful life" but that at his time of writing (1908) the spirit had long since "returned to his old victim in whose presence and through whose personality he is now, the 'invisible terror' of the neighbourhood in which he lives." Bob MacNeill, according to Hubbell, was now forever burdened with the evil astral body that had haunted Esther. Hubbell went on to boast that one day scientists would turn to his hypothesis to solve, once and for all, the question of the supernatural.

While Hubbell was confident in his abilities as an investigator and a theorist, many and varied opinions expressed about the Mystery received equal coverage in the press.

The Esther Cox case intensified the rivalry between two local newspapers, which took turns accusing the other of sensationalizing the story to improve its circulation. And while the *Chignecto Post* and *Amherst Gazette* lost no opportunity to report the goings-on at both 6 Princess Street and White's Oyster Saloon, their editorial staff took offence to any suggestion from their peers that they believed Esther Cox was the victim of evil spirits or any other aspect of the supernatural. On November 7, 1878, the *Post* wrote an editorial entitled "The Cox Phenomena" as a supplement to the statements of both Dr. Carritte and the Reverend Temple. The *Post* drew fire due to its extensive coverage of the Mystery and was attempting to explain why it had done so. It called the words of Carritte and Temple "plain straightforward statements of fact," which led one to conclude that "these manifestations result from natural causes, from electricity or some kindred force." The *Post* set itself up in contrast "to a portion of the press" that "in its zeal for sensationism" endeavoured to coat the Cox case with "supernatural glamour." The editorial went on to say that, while a great number of mysteries in this world, such as thunder and lightning, had puzzled great minds for centuries, their cause was now known. It scoffed at the idea of evil spirits capable of breaking God's laws of nature, and blamed publications like the *Banner of Light*, a promoter of spiritualism, for publishing "endless repetitions of infinite twaddle." The *Chignecto Post* believed that Esther's manifestations could be explained through the phenomenon of electricity.

On November 8, the *Amherst Gazette* took credit for breaking the Esther Cox story in the first place and stated that "some of the city papers are just beginning to wake up to the fact that Amherst has had an unusual phenomenon, whereas it was first made public through a lengthy article in the *GAZETTE* two months ago" when it described Esther as a "medium of the magnetic influence."

On November 14 the *Post* shot back at a supposed criticism with, "The *Telegraph* [presumably referring to the *Saint John Daily Telegraph*] says we admit there is 'something' in the Cox manifestations. Of course we do. We admit there is something in the small-pox, measles or cholera morbus, but we do not know there is anything very supernatural about those complaints, nor do we believe there is anything supernatural about the Cox affair. If the *Telegraph* means that that 'something' is supernatural we distinctly repudiate the assumption. We have no desire to be placed in that class of credulous idiots, who run crazy over every new sensation, or are led away by every new whim of doctrine." The *Post* defended publishing what it did about the case, claiming only "the sole desire to rob the affair of the air of mystery and superstition that a portion of the press seemed determined to invest it." It ended by declaring that "the *Telegraph* in giving undue weight and prominence to this affair has certainly catered to the morbid and unhealthy taste of the people, a course which cannot be too strongly deprecated." On November 9, the *Saint John Daily Telegraph* quoted the *Amherst Sentinel* as saying, "too much has been made of the Amherst Mystery. It was mostly moonshine."

The *Chignecto Post*, however, kept printing stories about Esther. On December 12, 1878, one of its reporters present during an episode at White's Oyster Saloon and convinced that the manifestations were genuine wrote, "if any one in Amherst doubted the fact of the manifestations taking place as described, there was no difficulty in setting them at rest pretty effectually." The paper also believed that the power came from within Esther, not from outside forces, in view of the statement of Esther's doctor, that he "could subdue the manifestations, by the administration of sedatives to Miss Cox." The *Post* did not believe that evil spirits could be driven away by medicine and saw this, along with Dr. Carritte's experiments that seemingly stopped the flow of electricity from Esther's body, as proof that "the force exerted came from her and not from any external source." The newspaper believed Dr. Carritte's actions "dissipated into the air high flown speculations as to their spiritualistic or mesmeric or demoniac origin."

During the newspapers' feud and their attempts to get their particular points across, little concern was shown for Esther, how she was feeling, or what she might be thinking. The *Post* was sympathetic to a point. On December 12 it stated that what was happening was "very harassing to herself" and was made more so by the fact that the medical profession, excepting Dr Carritte, of course, did not seem to have any remedy for her. The *Post* felt that the case was worthy of consideration by the best medical minds of the day and hoped that Esther "will be placed where her case can be the most advantageously studied."

By the spring of 1879 the story had found its way to newspapers outside the Maritimes. On May 15, 1879, the *Chignecto Post* reported that the "Esther Cox phenomena are set down by the *Montreal Gazette* as a humbug and a fraud." The *Post* jumped to the defence of its local heroine by asking "is it not better for scientists to examine the cause of this mysterious force, instead of standing off and pooh-hoohing its existence?"

Hubbell was correct when he predicted that his hypothesis concerning ghost stories such as the Great Amherst Mystery would be examined by others. The first to do so was Hereward Carrington, the paranormal researcher with the American Society of Psychical Research, who visited Amherst and then Brockton in 1907. Carrington had read Hubbell's book and was interested in learning more about the case. Although he lamented the absence, through relocation or death, of a good number of the eye witnesses to the manifestations, he was able to garner a couple of new stories from the Teeds about what had occurred in the house during Esther's stay there. More important, however, was Olive's admission to Carrington that "she had never seen an object start on its journey through the air, and, never actually saw it in the air. It had invariably finished its journey when she observed it." Olive also told Carrington that she felt that in places Hubbell had "dramatized and embellished" the manifestations. Despite Olive's disclaimers and the cold reception he received from Esther and her husband, Peter, Carrington was convinced that Hubbell had been correct in his assessment of the situation, and that Esther had indeed been haunted by supernatural forces.

Twelve years later, however, the findings of both Hubbell and Carrington received a scathing rebuke from Dr. Walter Franklin Prince, another student and investigator of the paranormal sciences. Prince was a former Episcopal minister who held a Ph.D. in divinity from Yale University, and developed, later in life, an interest in abnormal psychology. Like Carrington, he was a research officer with the American Society of Psychical Research, and during his career had investigated many cases of supposed supernatural activity.

Although Prince never did a first-hand investigation into the Great Amherst Mystery, he certainly held some definite opinions on the subject. In "A Critical Study of The Great Amherst Mystery," published in the August 1919 issue of the *Proceedings of the American Society for Psychical Research*, he stated that "nobody has hitherto seemed to find time to look into the 'Great Amherst Mystery' with a critical eye." He deemed the case worthy of such study as it "has become in its way a classic." He cast a jaundiced eye on the findings of Walter Hubbell, whom he perceived as concerned only about the monetary gain that Esther's plight offered him. Prince found Hubbell's arguments to be deeply flawed, citing among his reasons the small number of eye witnesses and the vagueness of their accounts, the divided opinions expressed about the case, which Hubbell fails to mention, and the uselessness of the "testamentary document" that the actor so highly prized.

Prince also cast doubt on Hubbell's self-touted expertise as an "investigator of the supermundane," calling him "more than ordinarily emotional" and claiming that his imagination was "resourceful to excess," not suitable traits for one formulating theories. Prince saw Hubbell's stage experience as getting in the way of his recording of events. He accused the actor of dramatizing incidents and conversations that occurred months before his arrival in Amherst. He brought Hubbell to task for adding to the notes he had initially written in 1879 as the years progressed, and expanding upon them in various editions of his books. Prince's lengthy article slowly picked apart Hubbell's personality, research, and recording abilities, leaving little of the actor's theories of the Mystery remaining in its wake.

In Walter Prince's opinion, "psychological abnormality" was behind the Great Amherst Mystery. He believed Esther's mental constitution was such that it could easily "disintegrate through shock and strain." Prince saw the shock to her system as brought about by what happened between her and Bob during the buggy ride and the strain of the following days when she was distraught over the incident. He believed that Esther's mind, in the effort to stop the bad memories, subconsciously created another personality, a personality unknown to the rational Esther, which produced noises, caused objects to move, and set fires. Prince, in short, diagnosed Esther as suffering from multiple personalities.

Despite Hubbell's failings as a theorist and recorder, he did, at least on one occasion, consider Esther's personality and state of mind when he asked Daniel Teed if she had "ever received a severe shock of any kind; such as news of sudden death, escape from instant destruction, or anything of a nature that would have been likely to affect her nervous system." It was then that he learned about the events of the buggy ride as related by Esther to her family:

> *Bob drove onto the marsh and into a small grove of trees. When they reached it Bob leapt down from the buggy and drew a large revolver from the side pocket of his coat, pointed it at Esther's heart and commanded her to get out of the buggy or else he would kill her where she sat. She was very much frightened of course, to leave the buggy, telling him to get in and drive her home, and not act like a madman. Her refusal to comply with his demand enraged him so, that he aimed at her heart again, uttering terrible oaths the while, and about to fire, when the sound of wheels was heard coming in their direction. It was now growing dark and raining. When he saw the wagon approaching he instantly returned to the buggy and drove her toward home at a break-neck speed in the now pouring rain.*

It was upon hearing this account that Hubbell surmised how the evil spirits had come to possess Esther. And when *The Haunted House* was published in 1879, everyone in Amherst and the surrounding area thought they knew what had happened between her and Bob MacNeill. Esther's life, in the minds of Amherst residents and the reading public, would be connected forever after to the supernatural. Whatever other names they had ascribed to Esther, she had without a doubt become a curiosity, a victim, and a shamed woman.

The editors of the *Wesleyan* were right: Esther Cox did indeed pose a problem for her family, doctors, clergymen, Walter

Lower Victoria Street, Amherst, circa 1895.

Hubbell, and the local papers. Their attempts to label her and to explain what happened during those fifteen months in 1878 and 1879 produced varied conclusions, but none satisfactorily defines Esther and her situation.

It is, moreover, the voices of men that are heard throughout this case, whether in Hubbell's pompous, self-congratulatory tone or in the quasi-scientific musing of local editorials. Esther herself is silent. Her only apparent words are heard through the filter of the Reverend Robert Temple and her brother-in-law Daniel Teed, and she has been forever marked as the helpless and hapless victim of Bob MacNeill. But while Esther Cox was indeed "rural, uneducated and unsophisticated," she was never totally without power, nor without the desire and ability to use it.

CHAPTER 7
A Haunted Girl

The impressions on her mind ought not to be cast aside in seeking the bottom of this mystery.
~ The Reverend Robert A. Temple

Without Walter Hubbell we likely would not know about Esther Cox today. But while his book, *The Haunted House*, did prevent her experiences from being lost, it also overdramatized events and portrayed her mainly as a victim and an oddity. Little of the real Esther can be found there.

Hubbell also played fast and loose with the facts. He says, "I have not permitted my imagination to so embellish the account as to distort it, nor in any way endeavoured to make it attractive at the expense of veracity." But Olive Teed told Hereward Carrington that "Hubbell had dramatized and embellished" his story in places. He also cast himself as the hero, declaring that it was he who taught Esther and the Teeds how to communicate with the spirits by knocking when, in fact, it was newspaperman J. Albert Black who introduced them to the concept. Hubbell also boasted that it was he alone who could have saved Esther from her jail sentence, stating that "judge and jury did not believe in ghosts, and I was not there to explain."

Hubbell placed Dr. Carritte at the scene when the threat "Esther Cox you are mine to kill" was scratched out on the bedroom wall. But the doctor himself, in the November 7, 1878, *Chignecto Post*, stated that "the writing on the wall and the matches setting fire to the house, I know nothing about." Hubbell also claimed that the medicine administered to Esther by Dr. Carritte was "neutralized by the ghosts" and had no effect on her, while Carritte said that he "could subdue the manifestations, by the administration of sedatives to Miss Cox."

Hubbell portrayed Esther, the Teeds, indeed the whole town of Amherst, as backwater rubes in need of his guidance. But they were more sophisticated than Hubbell admitted. They knew how to conduct a seance and were familiar with mesmerism and spiritualism long before he came along. And while he sets himself up as a man of the world, his arguments and observations often come off as comical and naïve.

Hubbell skimmed over the end of the manifestations of the Great Amherst Mystery, telling his readers that a Mi'kmaq medicine man performed an exorcism on Esther. There were Mi'kmaq living in and around Amherst at the time and their spiritual leaders did conduct ceremonies in order to chase away evil spirits. But Hubbell supplied no further details about the exorcism, such as the name of the person performing it or where it was done. And the local newspapers, always so eager to print any news of Esther, reported no such ceremony. It is highly unlikely, in any case, that staunch Christians like Daniel and Olive Teed, or Esther herself, would have sought assistance from outside their own spiritual faith.

We need to look elsewhere for a solution. What caused the manifestations of the Great Amherst Mystery to stop? And, more important, what caused them to start? There are alternatives to

Hubbell's explanation of the supernatural. Some can be found in other stories of hauntings and supernatural possession similar to Esther's.

Perhaps the best-known incident of possession in North America occurred in 1692 in the Massachusetts Bay Colony and led to the Salem Witch Trials. Winters in Salem Village were long and boring for everyone. Unmarried girls, in particular, had few social diversions apart from attending church. In January 1692, a number of them began to gather in the kitchen of the Reverend Samuel Parris's home. Tituba, Parris's elderly servant, originally from Barbados, entertained the girls with stories of voodoo spells and fortune telling.

As the weeks went by, some of the girls began to act strangely. They had convulsive fits, some got down on all fours and barked like dogs, others complained of a choking sensation in their throats. They had hallucinations and claimed they were being pinched and bitten, and often they had the marks to prove it. They kicked, they screamed, they refused to do their chores. Although the recurring episodes always passed with no lasting effects, parents were at their wits' end. They called in Reverend Parris and other church officials for help.

The first question the girls were asked was, "Who has bewitched you?" The youngsters were surprised at first, but then started naming names, claiming that a number of older women in the community were witches who had cast a spell on them. The Salem Village Witch Hysteria was sparked. It lasted less than a year but resulted in the deaths of twenty-five innocent people.

While the hysteria went on, the girls continued their convulsions, accusing their neighbours and testifying against them in court while writhing on the floor and fainting. They were fussed over by their parents and consulted by church authorities. One word from them could mean life or death. They were both feared and respected. Previously, it had been the community elders who told people what to do and what to think. Now the tables were turned and the girls were having the time of their lives. Soon, other young women in surrounding communities, including Salem Town and Beverley, were experiencing similar physical ailments and accusing local matrons of witchcraft.

Many theories, besides witchcraft, have been put forth as to the cause of the girls' symptoms, such as mass hysteria, a hallucinogenic fungus, and poisoning. But the likeliest explanation lies elsewhere. The citizens of seventeenth-century Salem Village believed in a merciless, Old Testament God. They were Puritans, and their lives revolved around the Calvinist church and its teachings. While they worshipped and feared a righteous and powerful God, they also believed in and feared the devil and witchcraft. The young girls' debilitating fears, belief in Tituba's stories, and the opportunity to usurp authority and gain attention were the underlying causes of the hysteria. Later, as older women, some of the afflicted girls apologized publicly for their accusations.

The case of a young girl who, like Esther, was thought to be a human battery appeared in the article "The Electric Girl of La Perrière" in the September 1864 issue of the *Atlantic Monthly*. The article's author, Robert Dale Owen, described Angélique Cottin as "a peasant-girl fourteen years old, robust and in good health, but very imperfectly educated and of limited intelligence" who lived with her widowed aunt in the tiny village of La Perrière, France. Angélique was dubbed "the electric girl" because it was believed that she had an overabundance of electricity in her body that caused objects to move about. It all started on January 5, 1846, when the loom around which she and three friends were working fell to the floor whenever Angélique touched it. The girls became frightened, and called for help. The frame was put back into place but when Angélique approached, it again crashed to the floor. The story quickly spread through the village that witchcraft was afoot.

Angélique's aunt consulted the local priest, who reassured her that the girl was not bewitched but had a "bodily disease." He referred Angélique to a local physician, Monsieur de Farémont, but the doctor could shed no further light on the matter. He did have his suspicions, however, and performed a variety of experiments on the girl, including using glass to control the supposed flow of electricity from her body. By now Angélique was causing chairs, dishes, and cutlery to move about of their own accord. People swarmed to the Cottin cottage to watch.

With an eye to financial gain, Angélique's father decided to take her to Paris, where people would pay a hefty fee to see her perform. Upon arrival there, she was examined by a committee of doctors and scientists, which concluded, from the erratic nature of her manifestations, that Angélique was a fake. Robert Owen related that the "attractive and repulsive phenomena, after continuing for upwards of a month, happened to cease at the very time the committee began to observe them." He suspected that to please her parents and to continue an act that had quickly gotten out of hand, the poor child "really did at last simulate phenomena that once were real." No longer able to attract an audience, Angélique and her family were left stranded in Paris. The electric girl phenomenon had lasted little more than a month.

In November 1868 the *Atlantic Monthly* published "A Remarkable Case of 'Physical Phenomena,'" about another young woman at the centre of mysterious circumstances. In the summer of 1868, Mary Carrick was a maid for a well-to-do Massachusetts family. She had emigrated from Ireland the year before and was described by H. A. Willis, the author of the piece, as "very ignorant, like most of her class, but quick to learn anything required."

The family (whose name was not disclosed) became aware that something was amiss with their servant in July when the summoning bells in the kitchen rang for no apparent reason. In the following days rapping noises were heard throughout the house, on the walls, doors, and windows, and chairs, crockery, tables, and kitchen utensils flew about whenever Mary was present. Willis was called in to investigate the matter. He tested Mary's bedstead for electrical currents and insulated it by placing the posts on sheets of glass. But the knocking sounds and flying objects persisted. Willis noticed that "these manifestations were much more frequent in rainy, wet weather than on sunny days," with the most "marked and violent demonstrations" taking place when the weather was bad. In the middle of the pandemonium, Mary left the house for a couple of days to get a rest. Nothing occurred while she was gone, but as soon as she returned the manifestations recommenced. In early September, after a particularly violent session of knocking and moving of furniture, the commotion ceased altogether and neither Mary nor the family was ever bothered by them again.

On September 12, however, Mary's "nervous system succumbed, and she was suddenly seized with a violent attack of hysteria." The girl continued to suffer from crying and nervousness until she was admitted to an asylum, where she stayed for three weeks. Mary returned to the family's employ, but was not able to stay. She took to sleepwalking and "complained of great distress in her head" and was again removed to the asylum.

Mary's employer was a large family of ten. One can assume that some of the members were children and teenagers. Her torment lasted for only ten weeks, beginning in July and perhaps coinciding with vacation from boarding school or university. Most of the occurrences took place on rainy days, when young gentlemen and ladies would be forced indoors with little to occupy their time. After reading Willis's article one cannot help but conclude that this poor servant girl, newly arrived in America, was the victim of neither spirits nor electricity, but of spoiled and bored youngsters who could easily have rung bells, knocked on walls, thrown utensils, and moved tables around a room without being detected. The manifestations lasted until early September, just when these young people would be returning to their studies. But for Mary Carrick, the "haunting" continued, with nervousness, headaches, sleeplessness, and institutionalization.

Even while Esther was in the midst of the Great Amherst Mystery, other strange occurrences were taking place in the Maritimes. On December 16, 1878, the *Saint John Daily Telegraph* carried a story entitled "A Halifax Mystery." While the identity of the family concerned was kept secret, the head of the household, "a sturdy and very muscular man, of middle age" was referred to as "Mr. M." He and his wife, along with their daughters, ages eighteen, twenty-two, and twenty-five, a twenty-year-old son, and two young male boarders, had resided in an apartment on the top floor of a two-storey rental property for three years without incident. Then, one evening around the beginning of September 1878, they had just gone to bed when they were awakened by a knocking at the front door. Mr.

M answered it and found no one there, but the knocking continued. He woke the rest of the household, all of whom said they too heard sounds that seemed to be coming from the house's outer wall.

The knocking continued throughout the next week, first at night, then in the daytime as well, and it seemed to be following two of Mr. M's daughters. Soon the sounds, like those at 6 Princess Street, were answering questions and keeping time with whistled tunes. And, as in Esther's case, inanimate objects began to move around on their own. Storage trunks piled themselves on beds, a parlour table turned upside down, and clothing flew from hooks. One evening a large rug followed someone downstairs. The apartment was in an uproar. Mr. M did not want to move out but changed his mind when, in all the excitement, a "severe illness produced upon his daughter, and his wife became prostrated from attending her."

While on the surface the M family's plight was similar to that of the Teeds, there is another interesting connection. Dr. Edwin Clay, who was so taken with the Great Amherst Mystery and who travelled about providing lectures on the subject, was Mr. M's family physician. It is easy to imagine Mr. M discussing the particulars of Esther's case with Dr. Clay, comparing them with his own experiences, and then relating the same to his wife and family. Some of the six young people living in the apartment might have taken it into their heads to imitate many of Esther's manifestations in order to amuse themselves at the expense of a gullible Mr. M. The *Post* article twice mentions that he was unwilling to vacate the apartment and seems to have resisted doing so for some time. What better way to compel the head of the household to move from overcrowded or unsuitable lodgings than to convince him that the place was haunted?

The article concluded by saying that no disruptions had yet occurred in Mr. M's new accommodations.

At least two other unexplained cases occurring simultaneously with the Great Amherst Mystery might have been outright copycats. In December 1878, the *Presbyterian Witness* told its readers that "more mysteries are reported including one in Preston [near Halifax] similar to the Amherst Mystery." And on January 9, 1879, the *Chignecto Post* announced that Matilda Williams, a sixteen-year-old girl "whose father, a respectable caulker, lives on Black Spring Road" in Portland, just outside Saint John, New Brunswick, "has developed the phenomena of spiritualism, so called." The *Post* went on to say that Matilda suffered from visions, and "can make most anything she touches a divining rod." The girl was regarded as a spirit medium who communicated with the dead through "rappings and voices." Matilda, however, claimed a power that Esther never did: the ability to heal the sick. She was alleged to have cured an epileptic, someone suffering from rheumatism, and her own ailing mother. The *Post* further stated that "the individuals so cured have full faith in Matilda's powers, and now fully believe in the beneficent power exercised on them by her." Like Esther, Matilda's actions drew scrutiny, and the report ended with the assurance that the matter would be fully explored, as it was "making a good deal of talk" and Matilda was being "interviewed in different ways by different persons."

All these cases contain elements similar to those of the Great Amherst Mystery—the unexplained knocking sounds, the movement of objects, the short duration of events, the young women who were the focus of the phenomena. And the supernatural was always identified as the cause. There is, however, another, more likely explanation: young people looking to escape boredom, have a bit of fun, or challenge their elders. While the Salem Witch Hysteria proved disastrous and Mary Carrick's story was a sad one, both started out as nothing more than harmless pranks fuelled by an interest in the supernatural.

Trickery should always be a consideration for those looking into supernatural phenomena. It certainly was for people like Dr. Carritte and Walter Hubbell, who observed Esther and who, even though they believed in the existence of supernatural possession, spiritualism, mesmerism, and electrical magnetism, were also aware of how susceptible they were to deception. The Reverend Robert Temple told the *Chignecto Post* he was "quite assured of the honesty and sincerity of Mr. and Mrs. Teed and Miss Cox, and that they would not willingly lend themselves to any imposture." But that did not prevent his "examining for myself and testing, as far as I was able, the manifestations in order to satisfy myself they were not the result of fraud or collusion."

Dr. Carritte stated, "I heard of these manifestations before I went to the house, and believed they were an idle talk till I witnessed them for myself. I do not believe I could have been deceived in my own sensations of hearing and seeing, or that many others could have been deceived." One day, however, he stopped at White's Oyster Saloon and tied Esther to a chair so he could be sure she was not the cause of the knocking sounds coming from under the floorboards. And to live up to his boast of being able to detect any sign of fakery, Walter Hubbell was constantly on the alert. During that first seance at 6 Princess Street, he "watched all the persons present, saw their hands and feet by the light of the coal-oil lamp."

While not all mediums were opportunists and many did believe in the reality of their powers, deception often went hand in hand with the practice of spiritualism or mesmerism. By the time Amherst was marvelling over the Great Amherst Mystery, the tricks of the supernatural trade were well established. Mediums who made a living conducting seances and telling fortunes had a variety of helpful techniques and props at their disposal. Telescopic reaching rods were used to move objects around a room and specially made footwear helped produce knocking sounds. The dim light levels in most nineteenth-century homes were a great aid as well. The number of oil lamps in a room varied and there were always dark corners. Just to be sure, it was always recommended that the lights be turned down during seances. A variety of visual clues from the audience also helped mediums to conduct a successful seance. A raised eyebrow, a smile, a nod, heightened emotions, and crying were all invaluable tools.

Often a medium who was new to a community would visit the local cemeteries to make note of relevant names and dates and any new gravestones. In the United States, mediums used the so-called Blue Books, which contained helpful information about local families and pertinent facts on those individuals most likely to attend seances. When a medium left town, any new information that she or he had gathered would be added to the books they left behind at the inns or hotels that they in turn recommended to each other.

By the 1880s, belief in spiritualism had waned, due partly to the many fraudulent cases brought to light over the years. In an attempt to maintain interest, the claims of many of its practitioners grew increasingly far-fetched. On November 3, 1881, the *Chignecto Post* reported on a St. Louis, Missouri, medium capable of bringing forth the spirits of George Washington, Julius Caesar, Moses, Napoleon, Joan of Arc, Captain Kidd, and Genghis Khan.

But the greatest blow to spiritualism was levelled by its most respected practitioners. The famous Fox sisters, after years of earning a good living conducting seances, confessed that they too had used trickery. Maggie, with Katie in attendance, demonstrated their secrets to an audience of two thousand at the New York Academy of Music on October 21, 1888. She showed the rapt crowd how knocking sounds could be produced and a doctor in attendance confirmed that they were made by the cracking of her big toes.

Maggie related how the first ghostly sounds heard in their Hydesville home were produced. The girls simply tied a string around the stem of an apple and bounced the fruit up and down on their bedroom floor. They originally did so to tease their mother who believed in ghosts and constantly talked about their new home being haunted.

Katie Fox soon discovered that she could make unusual sounds with her fingers and by knocking her toes against the head- or footboard of the bed. After much practice, the girls also used their ankles, wrist joints, and elbows to produce rapping sounds. When success led the Fox sisters to public appearances, their secrets included throwing tiny lead pellets against the walls and ceiling, and attaching lead weights to their voluminous skirts.

Maggie Fox later recanted her confession, but it was too late. While spiritualism did continue, its reputation had suffered a major blow. Maggie and Katie Fox quietly slipped into obscurity, dying alone and in poverty.

So was there trickery involved in the Great Amherst Mystery? The descriptions of the manifestations found either in Hubbell's book or in the local papers are so vague it is difficult to tell what was really happening. Many are highly exaggerated and some events likely never occurred at all. Noises are described as loud, but how loud were they? Objects flew through the air and fell from the ceiling, but from which direction? And did they actually fly? Why was nothing ever seen moving from its starting place, only observed when it was landing, or at a standstill, in another location? How fast and how far did objects move? Witnesses were present when incidents occurred, but how many and, more important, who was not there? Esther's body swelled up. How much? How often? She lapsed into trances. How long, and to what degree? These are all questions vital to understanding exactly what happened, but there is no way they can ever be answered.

What is certain is that every reported manifestation of the Great Amherst Mystery, whether the movement of objects, the setting of fires, the cuts on Esther's body, the knocking sounds, or the writing on the walls, is an activity within the capabilities of human beings. Nothing happened to or around Esther that required anything beyond human strength and ability. No one but she saw the spirits or heard them speaking. And the discriminate and convenient appearances, or absences, of the manifestations according to time and place, and their abrupt and unexplained termination calls for an interpretation beyond the supernatural. In addition, while in late nineteenth-century Nova Scotia the possibility of ghostly spirits tormenting a young woman may have appeared, at least to some, as worthy of consideration, today Esther's problems would quickly catch the attention of social service organizations. Looking at Esther's situation through twenty-first-century eyes, most would assume that the source of the Great Amherst Mystery was human. And since Esther was the focus of the manifestations, she should be looked to for the key to their existence.

Downtown Amherst, circa 1895.

Indeed, it is reasonable to assume that it was Esther and Jennie Cox who created the Great Amherst Mystery in their bedroom. Like the Fox sisters before them, their interest in the supernatural led them to experimentation. After practicing awhile with threads or strings tied to that box of quilt patches, they were able to move it about. Soon they shared their abilities with William Cox and John Teed, and perhaps solicited the young men's help in performing other feats. It is likely that William and John partook, to some degree, in these deceptions as a lark and to get a reaction from Daniel and Olive. Their physical strength would have been an asset in producing the loud knocking sounds on the walls, roof, and in the cellar, and their absence from Esther's bedroom during her episodes would not have been noticed as much as would Jennie's. The four likely had a set of signals they used to communicate surreptitiously with each other.

It is particularly interesting to note that there is no mention of the pounding sounds on the roof of 6 Princess Street during or after Hubbell's stay at the Teeds', a time which coincides with John and William having moved away. While the young men likely played some role in producing the manifestations of the Great Amherst Mystery, their leaving curtailed these activities.

What Esther and Jennie started quickly got out of hand. It is one thing to startle your family, it is quite another to impress a public audience. John and William had to be careful that no one noticed them knocking on the sides of the bedroom wall with their knuckles or saw them going up into the attic or down into the cellar, where they pounded on the ceiling and floorboards with a hammer or maul.

And what about the chairs, dish pans, and scrubbing brushes that followed Esther around? Dr. Walter Prince wisely observed that these items always moved toward Esther, never away from her. Depending upon weight and stability, it is quite easy to get an object to follow you—just tie something to it and drag it behind you. In Esther's day, household thread, whether cotton, linen, or coarse silk, was much stronger than it is now. Thread used for creating buttonholes was often waxed, which added to its strength. Fishing line made of horse hair or cat gut, strong and virtually invisible, could also be used.

Esther also had access to the thread used in making shoes. Daniel, John, and William likely brought it home from the Amherst Boot and Shoe Company. Amherst historian John McKay remembers that the waxed thread used by his grandmother, also an employee of the Amherst Boot and Shoe, was strong enough to tow a truck. Such thread, tied around the ankle, wrist, or waist of a young woman, could easily have hauled around a few chairs and a scrubbing brush.

Once Esther's story got out, it would not have been hard for her to solicit the help of others who wished to join the fun—people like thirteen-year-old Fred, the son of John White, whose knife supposedly drew blood from her back. John White himself, eager to attract customers to his oyster saloon, might have assisted her. Since Esther was being closely watched, especially when in public, she needed help and there would have been no end of willing accomplices. Even without her solicitation or knowledge, some of White's young male patrons likely got into the act, making knocking sounds and throwing objects around. But none of Esther's human helpers ever got the credit for the havoc they caused. Instead, Esther laid the blame on the six spirits that she claimed were haunting her. The most powerful and ferocious of these was Bob Nickle, a sixty-year-old shoemaker who, Esther and Hubbell claimed, was the cause of most of the fires, moving objects, and loud knockings.

Esther said she was also followed by the spirit of Bob's sister Jane. Neither a Bob nor a Jane Nickle is listed in any Nova Scotia vital statistics records. Esther likely gave her spirit the name "Bob Nickle," because it sounds similar to Bob MacNeill. She also named one of her ghosts Eliza MacNeill, for one of Bob's older sisters, Eliza (MacNeill) Porteous, who was very much alive and a twenty-eight-year-old wife and mother living in Malagash at the time of the Great Amherst Mystery.

The spirit of one of Daniel Teed's distant relatives, Peter Teed, was also accused of haunting Esther. She described him as the best behaved of the lot, and said he often admonished the other spirits when they got too rambunctious. On November 12, 1848, Peter Teed, of Wallace, Nova Scotia, perished in a barn fire. Esther would have known of him from hearing family stories about his violent death.

The spirits of Maggie and Mary Fisher were supposedly those of two girls from Stewiacke. Esther quoted Maggie as claiming that "she died at age twenty-one years, had been dead twelve years and was now in hell. Her sister Mary had been dead three years and was nineteen years old when she died." Again, no one matching these descriptions has been found in the province's vital statistics. Esther's mother's maiden name was Fisher, so it is possible that the girls were relatives whom Esther had known about.

While Esther might truly have believed she was haunted, it is more likely that these particular spirits of the dead were figments of her imagination, created to add drama, elicit sympathy, and to blame for her actions. It is only in Hubbell's book that we learn the names of Esther's spirits. But in two newspapers items, we read of Bob MacNeill himself "haunting" Esther, once when she claimed that he hovered above her bed brandishing a knife, and again when she stated that she heard his voice imploring her to marry him.

The manifestations that Esther said were caused by the spirits were surprisingly predictable. During Hubbell's stay with the Teeds, they would "commence about 8 am and continue until 12 pm recommence about 1:30 pm and cease about 6 pm." They also were not active on Sundays. Indeed, the ghosts appear to have kept the same work hours as Daniel, who would not have been as amused as Hubbell was over a missing sugar bowl lid or flying umbrellas. Esther knew that Daniel could be pushed only so far.

It is also interesting that whenever Esther first relocated to another house, the manifestations did not occur right away. Hubbell's explanation was that it took the spirits a while to find her. It was more likely that Esther herself needed time. When arriving in a new home, she needed to get the lay of the land—to become familiar with the house and its inhabitants. Once Esther got used to a new routine and a new physical space, and found out whether the Whites, the Van Amburghs, or the Davidsons were sympathetic to her and believed in ghosts, she would start the manifestations again.

But the Great Amherst Mystery was much more than a series of slapstick comedy routines. Esther experienced attacks on her body. She was stuck with pins, scratched with knives and steak bones. She swelled up and cried in agony. She claimed she was surrounded by spirits who wanted to harm her, and she believed that Bob MacNeill had her under his spell. So what else was going on?

The Reverend Temple's remark in the *Chignecto Post* that Esther's state of mind might hold the key to the Great Amherst Mystery was insightful and sympathetic. Esther had likes and dislikes, hopes and dreams. She made choices, good and bad, in order to navigate through her world, and, like us all, she was a product of her environment. To understand Esther better, we need to look at the society in which she was raised and take into consideration what we know of her childhood and her life leading up to the events of the Mystery.

We all have expectations placed upon us by society and family, and this was certainly the case in Esther's time. By the nineteenth century in the Western world, society and religion had long since established that women were best suited to being wives, mothers, and homemakers. The "ideal" female was gentle and refined, sensitive and loving. She was the guardian of religion and morality. Thought to have a lower sex drive than men, women were held responsible for male sexual behaviour. The aggression and self-assertion encouraged in men were deemed to be inappropriate female traits. If women did venture out into the world with expectations of employment or living independently, an unbalance was sure to occur in their emotional, psychological, intellectual, and physical makeup. The only way to preserve a woman's gentle nature and reputation was to keep her at home.

This belief that the house was the proper sphere for women was preached from pulpits and written about in newspapers and popular ladies' magazines. It coincided with the belief that a man whose wife had to work was a failure.

While many nineteenth-century women lived obediently, even flourished under these ideals of womanhood, a small number rebelled, leaving their husbands, taking lovers, protesting for women's and animal rights or against poverty and slavery. The majority, however, took the middle road, living within these constraints, but making a life for themselves. They wrote, painted, or pursued a variety of hobbies. The unmarried sought employment as teachers or housekeepers.

There was, however, another option for women during this time, which permitted them, consciously or not, to rebel against the demands of their lives while avoiding outright defiance. That option was hysteria.

Women were believed to be more susceptible than men to sickness and disease. This often proved a means to escape from day-to-day responsibilities or an unfulfilling life. Women took to their beds with a variety of complaints, including fatigue, palpitations of the heart, seizures, uncontrollable crying or laughing, convulsions, loss of appetite, trances, and hallucinations. Often, doctors could find no physical source for these ailments, which could be brought on by events such as a death in the family or a financial setback, but would diagnose the problem as "hysteria," a temporary loss of control over the emotions.

Haunted Girl

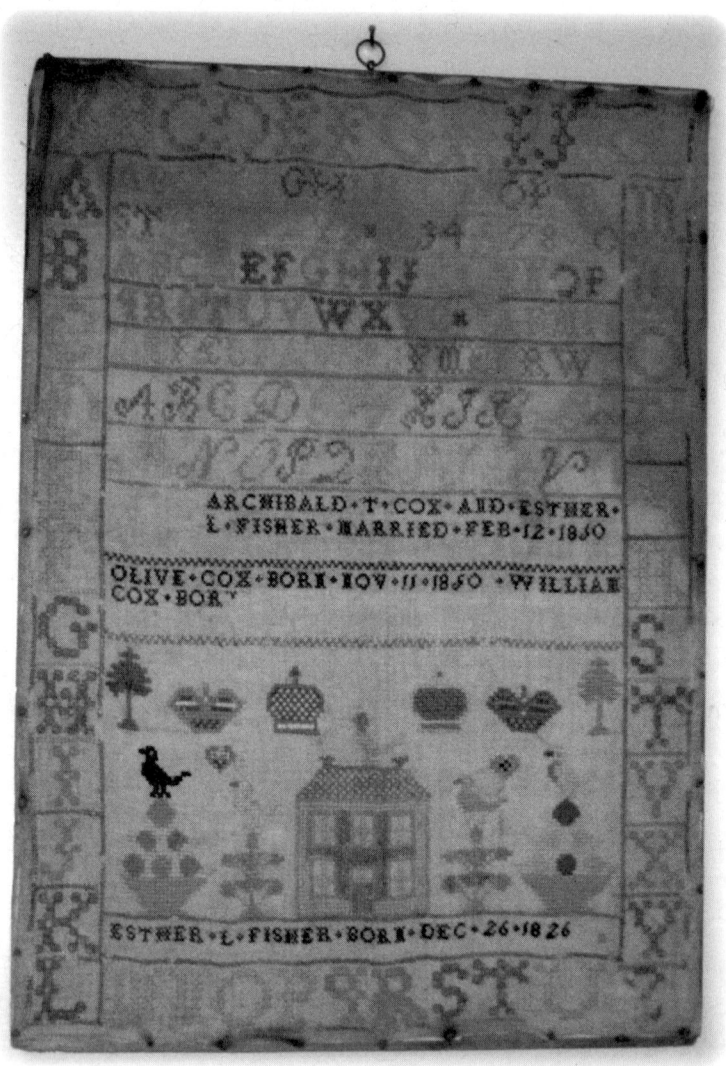

Sampler owned by Esther (Fisher) Cox, Esther's mother.

Because hysteria was considered a disease, its victims were treated as invalids, with their wants and needs taking centre stage. They stayed in bed and were catered to by family members and friends, who took over their responsibilities.

Although Esther's troubles were not referred to as hysteria, many of her symptoms were similar. Described by Dr. Carritte as suffering from "nervous prostration," she experienced convulsions during which her stomach, arms, and legs swelled up. She went into trances and had hallucinations in which she claimed to see her dead mother. Most of Esther's "illness" took place during the night, while at home. There are no references to her going through convulsions or trances while at the White, Van Amburgh, or Davidson residences, but she did become "ill" in Moncton after the failed presentation at Ruddick's Hall. During the day, Esther's complaints were of a more supernatural nature: she claimed the spirits had slapped, scratched, cut her, and stuck her with pins.

Today, many of those nineteenth-century women who suffered from hysteria would be diagnosed with depression. Esther herself likely suffered from a generalized anxiety disorder. Many of her symptoms certainly are the same as those commonly listed for anxiety, such as a tingling or burning sensation on the skin, tremors and shaking, panic attacks, and heart palpitations. Esther also might have had an underlying physical condition that brought on some of these problems, such as lupus, which can cause numbness and tingling of the skin, or a kidney condition that, depending on one's stress level, can lead to elevated blood pressure and body swelling.

On a number of occasions, Dr. Carritte gave Esther laudanum, the side effects of which include irritability, itchiness, constipation, depression, nausea, dry mouth, and loss of appetite.

Laudanum is highly addictive, and Esther may also have suffered withdrawal symptoms between Carritte's visits.

Esther's problems, however, likely went deeper than the physical. It is possible that she suffered from any number of psychological disorders which, so many years later, would be impossible to identify for certain. While there is no way to know for sure what these disorders were, they can, however, be speculated upon. We can begin with the assumption that Esther was straining under a considerable amount of anxiety.

Anxiety is brought on by psychological stress. What were Esther's stresses and where might they have originated? Esther certainly experienced abandonment early in life. The loss of her mother, at the age of three weeks, was likely too early to make a lasting impression on her, but the separation from her siblings, her father's two remarriages, and his absence for most of her young life would have helped to create a fear of further abandonment that could have lasted into adulthood. In addition, Esther was the youngest in the Cox family and her birth likely contributed to her mother's death. Her father and older siblings might have blamed her, directly or not, for that death, and Esther may have carried the guilt of it with her.

Along with her fear of abandonment, Esther may have feared her own death. Both her mother and stepmother had died, and she would have heard stories about her sister Abigail, who had also passed away. As a child Esther likely feared for her own life as well as those of other family members.

Esther was raised by her grandparents. Sometimes, whether they are protective or not, grandparents can be more permissive than parents. Such permissiveness, when coupled with punishment, encourages narcissism in children. We all have a narcissistic stage, from about three to six years of age. While most of us outgrow it and go on to other developmental stages, some people never do, forever remaining self-focused. Those with narcissistic personalities have a deep craving for attention and an equally deep fear of rejection. They will do whatever it takes to secure the first and avoid the other, including crossing boundaries between appropriate and inappropriate behaviour.

Modern psychology has identified a specific personality type as borderline. Individuals with borderline tendencies have no sense of self, so they demand time and attention from others. They are often angry about what is happening in their lives and blame others for it. They feel entitled, they want their own way, they lie, and they never accept blame.

Walter Hubbell's description of Esther's behaviour, if accurate, is telling. He writes that at times she could "be very self-willed, and likely to have her own way when her mind was set on anything. If asked to do some thing she did not feel inclined to do, she would become sulky, and often had to be humoured to keep peace in the family." If the Teed family had to tiptoe around Esther when she was upset, it is a good indication that she did have a strong personality, and was resentful and demanding. And while she may simply have been behaving like any spoiled teenager, in light of what else was happening in her life during this period, it can be assumed that Esther was suffering from some deeper, underlying problems. Her behaviour, as much as can be known of it at this point, is similar, in some respects, to individuals with narcissistic tendencies and borderline personality.

Of course, there are just too many unknowns about Esther's life for anyone to identify with certainty the reasons for her actions, or indeed, exactly what those actions were. As a young child she may have, as many children do, indulged in fantasy and continued the practice into early adulthood in order to escape the painful or mundane reality of her own existence. Some form of abuse may have played a formative role during her early years. Esther could also have been a person who craved variety and adventure and turned to the supernatural to fill that need.

So for Esther—with her childhood behind her, and perhaps with a fear of abandonment, a craving for attention, a desire to escape reality, and a lack of appropriate boundaries firmly in place—the prospect of living in Daniel's and Olive's crowded home, complete with its duties and expectations, would not have been a pleasant one. By September 1878, Esther likely was unhappy with her situation as everyone else was getting on with their lives. Olive had a husband and two children, Jennie was the pretty one with a steady job, and Nellie had just gotten married and moved away. Daniel, William, and John were men whose meals had to be cooked and clothes had to be washed. The children, Willie and George, were the centre of attention in the household. Where was Esther's place in all this? What did she have to call her own? She had been sure that the handsome Bob MacNeill was going to propose to her, but he had not—in fact, he had left town altogether. She had likely considered him to be her only chance for marriage and a home of her own, and now that hope was gone as well.

Esther may well have viewed her move into a house that was not her own, and where she had to cook for and clear up after others, as a loss of status that she needed to regain. Consciously or unconsciously, she would quickly have built up resentment and looked for ways to act out, challenge authority, and gain attention. That attention could be positive or negative; it would not have mattered much to Esther.

Her convulsions, flying bedclothes, mysterious knocking sounds, and evil spirits soon provided her with more attention than she had bargained for. She became the number one concern at 6 Princess Street. People gathered at her bedside asking questions and waiting for something to happen. Her name appeared regularly in the newspapers. She received invitations to travel, appeared on stage before hundreds of people, and had a book written about her. In short, she became a celebrity. But this desired attention was accompanied by inner conflict, a conflict made visible in physical self-abuse and the lighting of fires.

Today, a number of young people, girls in particular, cut their bodies with razors, knives, or other sharp objects. They do it as a self-punishment, for release from psychological pain, and to express anger. While those who injure themselves in this way usually hide their wounds, Esther claimed that she was the victim of evil spirits, making it more acceptable to speak about and display hers.

Esther's forehead was cut with a steak bone. Fred White's jackknife was stuck into her back at White's Oyster Saloon. Esther told Hubbell that the spirits tried to cut her throat with a carving knife and stab her in the neck with shears. On one occasion she was stuck with pins. Esther, along with Jennie, showed Hubbell the small crosses scratched into her body. All these incidents would have caused considerable physical pain—pain, self-punishment, and relief from anxiety, but they were also a device for eliciting sympathy and attention.

Setting fires is also a cry for help and a sign of inner turmoil. The fires at 6 Princess Street originated in Esther's bedroom and in the cellar, two locations where she could be alone, unobserved by the rest of the family. These fires threatened her physical safety along with that of her immediate family and

Amherst's downtown core, yet she could not help herself. This behaviour reached its climax with the fires in the two barns, Esther's arrest for arson, and her ultimate public humiliation: incarceration.

All this behaviour—the cutting, the fires, the moving furniture, the knocking, the profane writing on the walls and the talking to spirits—served to disrupt and to shock. The uncertainty as to what was going to happen next left the Teed family virtually at Esther's mercy. She constantly, whether consciously or not, undermined any attempt to provide a sense of normality in the household. Such unpredictability was a way for her to challenge Daniel and Olive without directly disobeying them.

When things got to be too much for the Teeds, Esther was removed from their home and, like a foster child, taken in by other families. She worked as a servant in these homes and likely was not paid as her presence at the Whites, the Van Amburghs, and the Davidsons would have been regarded as a favour to Daniel. Nonetheless, it was Esther who controlled the length of time she stayed away from 6 Princess Street. Hubbell tells us that she found her first stay at the Van Amburghs' tedious and returned to Amherst "having become weary of the dull life she was compelled to lead in the woods."

During this time Esther would have been experiencing a range of conflicting emotions. While she was finally getting the attention her personality demanded, she would also have felt guilty about her actions and notoriety when she remembered all the things her Grandmother Dickey had taught her about proper female behaviour. Her relationship with Bob MacNeill would have been particularly powerful in bringing these guilty feelings to the forefront.

There are a number of possible scenarios for what happened between Bob and Esther during their fateful buggy ride. It could have been one of many outings they had taken together or the first. She and Bob might have had consensual sex that night, for the first time or not. Bob might have raped her or assaulted her in some way—perhaps even, as Hubbell described, pulled a gun on her—any of which would have been traumatic and frightening. She might have been convinced that she was under his spell and believed him when he told her, "Esther Cox, you are mine to kill." He also could have merely informed her that he had been fired from his job or had simply decided to leave both the Boot and Shoe and the town of Amherst behind. Perhaps the buggy ride was his special way of saying his private goodbyes to her. Bob's behaviour and his leaving Amherst, for whatever reason, would have been seen as an abandonment by Esther, one of many that she had suffered. She might have truly cared for Bob and hoped that they would marry, giving her a status on par with that of Olive and Nellie. Whatever happened that evening, it was the last straw for Esther.

On September 12, 1878, fifteen days after the buggy ride, Esther's bodily convulsions began. Her stomach and limbs swelled, and her skin burned. Perhaps they were the psychosomatic results of the conflict and guilt she may have felt over some aspects of her relationship with Bob, which had been at odds with what she knew to be ladylike behaviour. If their relationship had been a sexual one, she might have felt guilty about having sex before marriage or feared she was pregnant. If Bob did assault her, in addition to the psychological and physical anguish that would have caused, she also could have felt guilt over "allowing" him to do so. Sometimes, during her convulsions Esther mimicked the motions of sexual intercourse, a telling indication both of inner turmoil and her knowledge of sexual acts.

Esther would have been enraged with Bob, whether he had raped her or simply decided to end their relationship. Whatever he did, he got away with it. She would also have felt anger at Daniel and the rest of her family for letting him "escape." If Daniel and Olive did believe that Bob had pulled a gun on Esther, or assaulted her in any way, there is no indication that they contacted the law to intervene, even though they knew his whereabouts. Esther would have resented them for not standing up for her, not attempting to right the wrong that had been done to her. She struck back, with the only option she had: the disruption of their lives.

Esther suffered greatly for her inappropriate, unladylike behaviour. She became a spectacle around town. Everyone knew what was going on in her bedroom, and they could not help but hear the strange sounds coming from the Teed house. After Hubbell's book was released, they knew about Bob MacNeill. They speculated and they gossiped. Esther was a one-woman sideshow, a curiosity stalked by spirits. She had been on the stage, a source of entertainment on the same level as actresses, who, at the time, were considered women of low morals and social standing. Worst of all, she had spent time in jail. She had been involved in things that no respectable person, certainly not a proper young lady, would dream of taking part in.

After the Mystery died down, and the doctors, the clergymen, and the curious were done with her, Esther would have been shunned by the very people who had clamoured to get inside the door of 6 Princess Street. In public, she would also have been a figure of fun and ridicule, with young boys shouting at her as she walked down the street. Her name would have been a warning to unruly children, their mothers telling them "to behave or Esther Cox will get you." Esther was shamed and no one—not the community, her family, or herself—would ever forget it. But she was more fortunate than some.

At the time there was an institution for the insane in Cumberland County. Referred to as the "lunatic asylum," it was likely situated in Pugwash. There was also a provincial institution, Mount Hope Asylum for the Insane, in Dartmouth. Many individuals displaying erratic and unusual behaviour spent time in one of these facilities. Luckily for Esther, she was regarded as "normal" enough to escape institutionalization. Dr. Carritte's interest in her as a scientific experiment and the belief that her troubles were not of her own making—physical rather than psychological—may have kept her from such a fate.

The manifestations surrounding Esther eventually did stop when she was arrested and put in jail. That was her wakeup call. She did have enough of a sense of self-preservation to realize that, at this point, things had gone too far and that she had to stop. Esther's awareness of how a proper young woman was to behave just could not be reconciled with being hauled into court and put in jail. As well, the rejection she expected to receive from her family and the community upon her release would be the ultimate humiliation for Esther and her fear of it was enough to cause her to abandon the supernatural.

Esther likely continued to act out in other inappropriate ways after her release from jail and her return to 6 Princess Street. She would have found herself right back in the same situation she had been in before her buggy ride with Bob. She still had to look after Willie and George and help Olive with the housework. She would still baulk when she had to do something she did not want to, and would still feel jealousy toward her sisters. But the Great Amherst Mystery, with its knocking spirits and turmoil, had run its course and had failed her. How Esther coped with her inner conflicts and fears for the rest of her life is not known.

Most of us—those not featured on daytime talk shows or reality television, at least—live our lives and experience our troubles and heartbreak in relative obscurity. Unfortunately for Esther, she became a celebrity, treated much as we treat the famous today, as curiosities whose every move fascinates. We long to have a connection with them, we envy them, and then we delight in their all-too-frequent downfall. The Great Amherst Mystery is not a story of ghosts and the supernatural but of a young, vulnerable, anxiety-ridden girl who craved attention and attempted to control her surroundings. Society's beliefs about women and about the supernatural during Esther's life and time, combined with the greed of an opportunist and her own psychological problems, turned her personal crises into a public sensation.

CHAPTER 8

The Legacy of the Great Amherst Mystery

*There are more things in heaven and earth, Horatio,
than are dreamt of in your philosophy.*
~ HAMLET ACT 1, SCENE 5

The Borley Rectory in the diocese of Chelmsford, Essex, was said to be "the most haunted house in England." Supposedly troubled by the ghosts of nuns and headless coach drivers since its construction in 1863, it experienced a particularly active period between 1930 and 1935 when the Reverend Lionel Algernon Foyster and his much younger wife, Marianne, were in residence. Windows shattered, bells rang, knocks resounded, writing appeared on walls, and objects flew through the air. British newspapers spread the story across the county and beyond. Harry Price, a self-appointed "psychic researcher" who lived in the Rectory for a time after the Foysters vacated it, wrote two successful books about its history and his time there.

After Rev. Foyster died, Marianne remarried and moved the United States. In the 1970s she was living in Philadelphia and when interviewed hinted that what happened at Borley Rectory during her life there had all been staged. Rev. Foyster was not a wealthy man and, wanting to leave his wife with a means of support after his death, he had brought the Rectory's haunted history up to date by creating a ghost that, he hoped, might bring them fame and fortune. Harry Price and his findings regarding the Rectory were later discredited as well.

The Borley Rectory haunting, interesting in its own right, takes on a whole new relevance when it is known that between 1927 and 1929 Rev. Foyster was rector of St. Paul's Anglican Church in Sackville, New Brunswick, situated a mere ten miles from Amherst. Canadian ghost-story writer John Robert Colombo believes that sometime during their stay in Sackville the Foysters read Hubbell's account of Esther's story. Like the M family in Halifax and Matilda Williams of Portland, New Brunswick, they were inspired to such a degree that they used it as the foundation on which to base their own supernatural experiences.

Walter Hubbell's book, *The Haunted House*, now entitled *The Great Amherst Mystery* has been reprinted many times. Its latest reissue was in 2009 as *The Great Amherst Mystery: An Eyewitness Account of the Most Famous Haunting of the Nineteenth Century* by the Texas-based Promethean Press. Although over one hundred years old, Hubbell's description of Esther's plight, continues to be the source of both information and debate for writers, researchers, and proponents of the paranormal.

Dr. Walter Prince was the first twentieth-century writer to take on Esther's case and although he refutes Hubbell's findings, his report did little to dispel people's belief that she was haunted by spirits of the dead. R. S. Lambert's *Exploring the Supernatural: The Weird in Canadian Folklore* accepts Hubbell's account as it stands and calls the Great Amherst Mystery "undoubtedly Canada's best ghost story." Peter Underwood in *Hauntings: New Light on the Greatest True Ghost Stories of the World* puts forth some alternative explanations for Esther's situation and clearly doubts Hubbell's story but still repeats the standard events of the case. It is writer Bruce Nunn's chapter on the Great Amherst Mystery in *Nova Scotia's Curious Connections: Stories of the Remarkable, the World-Famous and the Strange* that is the first, besides Prince's report, to seriously question the actions of both Esther and Hubbell.

There have been two fictionalized accounts of the Great Amherst Mystery. In *Mine to Kill*, author David St. Clair invents dialogue, elaborates upon events, and creates a happy ending for Esther and ghostly destruction for Bob MacNeill. William Meikle's recent ebook, *The Haunting of Esther Cox*, rehashes the whole story through fabricated diary entries

Esther's plight has also appeared on stage, where unique occurrences during two local productions did little to dispel her mystique. In 1991, *Guilty! The Story of the Great Amherst Mystery* was first performed by Sackville's Live Bait Theatre Company. Its sympathetic portrayal of Esther places her at the mercy of an unscrupulous Bob MacNeill, mischievous ghosts, and unforgiving judge and jury. In the middle of one of its performances, a raging electrical storm caused the building's lights to go out; the actors carried on in the dark to the heightened amusement of the audience. In 2001, the Tantramar Theatre Company of Amherst produced *Hangmen, Henchmen and Notables* in which a silent "Esther Cox" sat in one corner of the stage while the other characters moved around her. One evening, towards the finale, she stood to sing and was immediately joined by a bat, not part of the cast, which got into the building, circled her head for the entirety of her performance, and then disappeared.

So far, no photograph of Esther has come to light, however there have been some attempts to recreate her image. Just inside its front door, the Stewiacke Valley Museum displays a large, stuffed fabric doll seated in a rocking chair. The sign around its neck identifies it as "Esther Cox Our Resident Ghost." And in 2009, the Downtown Amherst Revitalization Society unveiled a colourful mural painted on a Havelock Street building that illustrates the key events of the Mystery, and features a larger-than-life image of Esther herself, undergoing her travails.

The Great Amherst Mystery is still very much part of the consciousness of Amherst and Esther remains a town celebrity. With the emergence of twenty-first century technology, knowledge of Esther Cox and the Great Amherst Mystery has gone global with versions of her story appearing on websites relating to ghost stories, poltergeist phenomena, and horror. In March 2010, Sins of a Saint, an Amherst-based metal band, posted their entry for the Great Amherst Song Contest on YouTube. Taking its lead from St. Clair's book, the song is entitled "Mine to Kill" and recounts Esther's plight.

During a 1989 radio interview, brothers Kent and Bill Leslie described the Canadian Tire store that their father managed as "the noisiest building in Amherst." Located on Prince Arthur Street, it covered a large area in downtown Amherst including the former site of 6 Princess Street. Its paint department was in the general location of Esther and Jennie's bedroom. The store was thought to be haunted, and unusual sounds were often heard by both staff and patrons. Kent told of how, when he was working alone one night, after store hours, he heard scuffling noises and whispers that were "unnerving and scary." He headed for the sports department, loaded a shotgun, and for an hour and a half stalked the store looking for intruders. Kent knew all the doors were locked and had no explanation for what he heard.

Bill Leslie then recounted how one evening when he was alone in the store there was "an ungodly crash in the warehouse area."

The Great Amherst Mystery mural, Havelock Street, Amherst, NS.

On going to investigate, he found that bales of sewer pipe, two or three hundred pieces of it, had come crashing down upon a counter. The pipe had been tied up in a large bundle with one-inch link chain but the chain had broken—in the middle—and the pipe tumbled down all over the place. "It was as if it unravelled itself and pulled apart," Bill stated. "Maybe it was the poltergeist that attached itself to Esther," he suggested.

What is it about Esther Cox and the Great Amherst Mystery that continues to fascinate so many over 130 years later? Most of us love a good, old-fashioned ghost story, but we are also attracted to that which cannot easily be explained.

In the nineteenth century, sensationalism played a huge role in the Great Amherst Mystery. Much about Esther Cox and the events she experienced was exaggerated to make a good story better, to gain attention, and for financial gain. But it is the Mystery's reputation as a ghost story that, while giving it notoriety and status within history and the horror genre, keeps it from being understood in other, more interesting ways. The Great Amherst Mystery has defined Esther Cox and determined how she is remembered today, but it was only one chapter of her life.

It was an interest in Esther Cox, the whole person, that inspired the writing of this book. Both Barb Thompson and I grew up with the story of the Great Amherst Mystery. But we knew little about it beyond that it was a ghost story, that the Canadian Tire store situated where the house once stood was haunted, and that the words "Esther Cox you are mine to kill" had mysteriously appeared on her bedroom wall.

Sharing a keen interest in women's history, we would, from time to time, discuss Esther, speculating about her personality and what the Great Amherst Mystery was really about. It was

Amherst in the 1880s. Photo by D. R. Pridham.

Barb's interest in what happened "after the mystery" and her research into Esther's life in Brockton, Massachusetts, that ultimately got this project underway. We knew there had to be more to Esther and we wanted to tell her entire story. Before, during, and after the Great Amherst Mystery, Esther Cox was, in turn, a daughter, granddaughter, and sister, a wife, mother, and grandmother. She was a hard worker and a contributing member of her community and her church. She was so much more than just "a haunted girl" and we wrote this book to reinterpret both her legacy and the historical record of her life in a way that will, we hope, bring dignity to her memory.

The story of Esther Cox and the Great Amherst Mystery as handed down to us by Walter Hubbell will continue to be read, repeated, and believed—it is, after all, a good ghost story. But to permit it to remain only a ghost story prevents so many other explanations from being considered. A new interpretation of the Great Amherst Mystery, one that demystifies Esther, and reveals her and her contemporaries as the complex individuals they were, seemed long overdue.

Acknowledgements

Thank you to the following for their assistance and helpful suggestions: Judith Colwell, Maritime Conference of the United Church of Canada Archives, Sackville, NB; Pat Crowe, Russell Fisher, Audrey Ryan, and Avery LeBlanc, Isabel Simpson Heritage Centre, Springhill, NS; Brenda Moore, Municipality of the County of Cumberland, Nappan, NS; Dr. Gail Campbell and Dr. Linda Kearly, Department of History, UNB, Fredericton, NB; Cathy Polson, Cumberland County Land Registration Office, Amherst, NS; Rob Gilmore and Twila Buttimer, Public Archives of New Brunswick, Fredericton, NB; Shirley Nickerson, Glenda Janes, and Christian Holiway, Cumberland County Museum and Archives, Amherst, NS; Philip Hartley, Public Archives of Nova Scotia, Halifax, NS; Carl Killen PC MLA for Saint John Harbour; Jeff Twine, American Society for Psychical Research, New York; Zofic Weaver, Society for Psychical Research, London, England; Carly Wright, Barbara Fisher, and Doug Beattie, Stewiacke Valley Museum, Stewiacke, NS; Felicity Osepchook and Jennifer Logan, New Brunswick Museum, Saint John, NB; Brenda Orr, Moncton Museum, Moncton, NB; Ann Flemming, Michelle Poor, Jane Fitzsimmons and Lucia Shannon, Brockton Public Library, Brockton, Mass.; Lee McBride, Porter Memorial Library, Machias, Maine; Kelly Nadal, McClelland & Stewart Ltd.; Dale H. Cook, USGen Web Project, Mass.; Nan

Harvey, Colchester County Historical Society Archives, Truro, NS; David Dewar, Wallace and Area Museum, Wallace, NS; Dale Swan, Tatamagouche Creamery Square North Shore Archives, Tatamagouche, NS; Jim Benson, President, Brockton Historical Society, Brockton, Mass.; North Cumberland Historical Society; St. Patrick's Church and Calvary Cemetery, Brockton, Mass.; Jan Sutherland, St. Colman's Catholic Church, Brockton, Mass.; Peter Seitl, Seitl's Antiques; Lorraine Roberts, South Shore Genealogical Society, Norwell, Mass.; Lorna Rodio; Marilyn Symons; Melanie Prendergast; Laurie Pennell Cooper; Don Miller; Dave March; Joanne Porter; James Bishop, Promethean Press; R. T. Van Pelt; Sylvia and Bill Fairbanks; Beth Munro and the Downtown Amherst Revitalization Society; and D. David Ward.

A special thank-you to the following individuals who lent their particular expertise to this book: Dr. Joan Wright, Clinical and Consulting Psychologist, Fredericton, NB; Carla Gunn, lecturer, Department of Psychology, Saint Thomas University; Dr. Margaret Conrad, Professor Emeritus, Department of History, UNB; Amherst historian John McKay; the Fictional Friends Writing Group: Kathie Goggin, Anne Leslie, Josephine Savarese, and Ana and David Watts. We are especially grateful to Sam Treen for leading us to Robert MacNeill's descendants.

Thank you to Patrick Murphy and Kate Kennedy of Nimbus Publishing: he for his confidence in this book that enabled us to tell Esther's story and she for her patience and sensitive editing of the manuscript. Thanks also to Whitney Moran for leading us over the finish line. It was a pleasure to work with Nimbus once again.

The descendants of the Cox, MacNeill, Clay, and Hubbell families gave generously of their time and information:

Tammy Smith, great-grandniece of Esther Cox; Tammy's daughter, Ainsley Smith-Gaudet; MacKean and Shelia Dickie (MacKean is a descendant of Olive Dickey); Guy Cox, great-great grandson of Archibald T. Cox; Eldon and Ian MacNeill, grandsons of Robert MacNeill; Penny Lane, great-grand niece of Robert MacNeill; Kathy Hufnal Martino, great-grand niece of Walter Hubbell; and Melanie Clay-Smith, a descendant of Dr. Edwin Clay.

Many thanks and much love to my husband, Barry Norris, for his continuing support and encouragement that keeps me writing.

It was Barb Thompson's initial research and desire to know what happened to Esther after 1879 that got this book started. Throughout the research and writing process Barb has always been there for me with wise counsel and humour. Thank you, my friend, for this adventure.

Any errors and omissions in this book are due entirely to the author's oversight.

Selected Bibliography

Appignanesi, Lisa. *Sad, Mad and Bad: Women and the Mind-Doctors from 1800*. Toronto: McArthur & Company, 2007.

Barrstadt, Carl, Michael Peterman, and Elizabeth Hopkins. "'A Glorious Madness': Susanna Moodie and the Spiritualist Movement." *Journal of Canadian Studies* 17, no. 4 (1982–83): 88–100.

Benson, James E. *Images of America: Brockton*. Chicago: Arcadia, 2010.

Brandon, Ruth. *The Spiritualists: The Passion for the Occult in the Nineteenth and Twentieth Centuries*. London: Weidenfeld & Nicolson, 1983.

Braude, Ann. *Radical Spirits: Spiritualism and Women's Rights in Nineteenth-Century America*. Boston: Beacon Press, 1989.

Brown, Harry R., et al. *Lore of North Cumberland*. Pugwash, NS: North Cumberland Historical Society, 1982.

Campbell, Bertha J., et al. *Springhill: Our Goodly Heritage, History, Happenings, Homes*. Springhill, NS: Springhill Heritage Group, 1989.

Carroll, Walter F. *Brockton from Rural Parish to Urban Center: An Illustrated History*. Northridge, CA: Windsor Publications, 1989.

Cohen, Daniel. "The Amherst Poltergeist." In *The Encyclopedia of Ghosts*. New York: Avon, 1984.

Colombo, John Robert, "Amherst/The Great Amherst Mystery." In *Mysterious Canada: Strange Sights, Extraordinary Events and Peculiar Places*. Toronto: Doubleday Canada, 1988.

———. "The Great Amherst Mystery Walter F. Prince." In *Three Mysteries of Nova Scotia*. Toronto: Colombo and Company, 1999.

Cook, Ramsey. *The Regenerators: Social Criticism in Late Victorian English Canada*. Toronto: University of Toronto Press, 1985.

Cox, Robert S. *Body and Soul: A Sympathetic History of American Spiritualism*. Charlottesville: University of Virginia Press, 2003.

Furlong, Pauline. *Images of Our Past: Historic Amherst*. Halifax, NS: Nimbus, 2001.

Guildford, Janet, and Suzanne Morton, eds. *Separate Spheres: Women's Worlds in the 19th-Century Maritimes*. Fredericton, NB: Acadiensis, 1994.

Gray, Charlotte. *Sisters of the Wilderness: The Lives of Susanna Moodie and Catharine Parr Traill*. Toronto: Penguin, 1999.

The Great Colliery Explosion of Springhill Nova Scotia, February 21, 1891. Springhill, NS: H.A. McKnight, 1891.

Hill, Joseph A. *Women in Gainful Occupations 1870 to 1920*. Washington, DC: US Government Printing Office, 1929.

Hubbell, Walter. *The Great Amherst Mystery*. Amherst, NS: Babineau Printing, reprinted 1982; originally published 1888.

———. *The Great Amherst Mystery: An Eyewitness Account of the Most Famous Haunting of the Nineteenth Century*. Dallas: Promethean Press, 2009.

———. *History of the Hubbell Family Containing a Genealogical Record Also Biographical Sketch, Deeds, Wills, Inventories. Distributions of Estates, Military Commissions, Obituaries, and much ancient Historical Information relating to the Family and Name*. New York: J. H. Hubbell, 1881.

Kaplan, Louis. *The Strange Case of William Mumler Spirit Photographer*. Minneapolis: University of Minnesota Press, 2008.

Killen, Joseph Carl. "William Nannery and Atlantic Victorian Theatre: The Amateur Legacy." M.A. thesis, University of New Brunswick, 1997.

Lambert, R.S. *Exploring the Supernatural: The Weird in Canadian Folklore*. Toronto: McClelland & Stewart, 1955.

Landers, Warren P., ed. *Brockton and Its Centennial: Chief Events as Town and City 1821–1921*. Brockton, MA: City of Brockton, 1921.

MacNab, Alexander. *The Pioneers of Malagash: Genealogical Record from Early Days*. Pugwash, NS: North Cumberland Historical Society, reprint 2007.

McKay, John G. *Esther's Ghosts: Mysterious Occurrences at 6 Princess Street Amherst N.S.* Amherst, NS: John McKay, 2010.

Miller, Thomas. *Historical and Genealogical Record of the First Settlers of Colchester County*. Truro, NS: Colchester Historical Museum, reprint 1991; originally published 1873.

Mitchinson, Wendy. *The Nature of Their Bodies: Women and Their Doctors in Victorian Canada*. Toronto: University of Toronto Press, 1991.

Morrow, R. A. H. *Story of the Springhill Disaster*. Saint John, NB, 1891.

Nunn, Bruce. *Curious Connections: Stories of the Remarkable, the World-Famous and the Strange*, 2nd ed. Halifax, NS: Nimbus, 2011.

Selected Bibliography

Owen, Alex. *The Darkened Room: Women, Power and Spiritualism in Late Victorian England*. Philadelphia: University of Pennsylvania Press, 1990.

Owen, Robert Dale. "The Electric Girl of La Perrière." *Atlantic Monthly*, September 1864, pp. 284–292.

Sherwood, Roland. "The Unsolved Mystery: Amherst." In *Maritime Mysteries: Haunting Tales from Atlantic Canada*. Hantsport, NS: Lancelot Press, 1976.

Smith, Cara L. "Personality Contributions to Belief in Paranormal Phenomena." *Individual Differences Research* 7, no. 2 (2009): 85–96.

Smith, James F. *Old Pugwash Families*. Hantsport, NS: Lancelot Press, 1985.

Smith-Rosenberg, Carroll. "The Hysterical Woman: Sex Roles and Role Conflict in 19th-Century America." *Social Research* 39, no. 4 (1972): 652–678.

St. Clair, David. *Mine to Kill*. London: Corgi, 1985.

Starkey, Marion L. *The Devil in Massachusetts: A Modern Inquiry into the Salem Witch Trials*. Alexandria, VA: Time-Life Books, reprint 1982; originally published 1949.

A Tale of Two Centuries: Truro Presbytery — Oldest in Canada. Truro, NS: Truro Presbytery History Committee, 1993.

The Town of Stewiacke, Nova Scotia. Truro, NS: Colchester Historical Society, 1967.

Tye, Diane. "Cox, Esther (Porter; Shannahan)." In *Dictionary of Canadian Biography Online*, vol. 14, *1911–1920*. Toronto: University of Toronto Press, 2000.

Underwood, Peter. "The Mystery of Amherst." In *Hauntings: New Light on the Greatest True Ghost Stories in the World*. London: J. M. Dent, 1977.

Ward, Peter. *Courtship, Love and Marriage in Nineteenth-Century English Canada*. Montreal; Kingston, ON: McGill-Queen's University Press, 2007.

Whittier, Henry Smith. *East Machias, 1765-1926*. Machias: University of Maine Press, reprint 1975; originally published 1927.

Wills, H.A. "A Remarkable Case of Physical Phenomena." *Atlantic Monthly*, August 1868, pp. 129–136.

Wilson Carpenter, Mary. *Health, Medicine, and Society in Victorian England*. London: Praeger, 2010.

Wojtczak, Helena. *Women of Victorian Sussex: Their Status, Occupations, and Dealings with the Law, 1830–1870*. Hastings, UK: Hastings Press, 2003.

Wright, Esther Clark. *Planters and Pioneers, Nova Scotia 1749–1775*. Hantsport, NS: Lancelot Press, 1982.

Selected Newspapers

Amherst Daily News, *Amherst Gazette*, the *Brockton Times*, *Chignecto Post*, the *Daily Times* (Moncton), the *Presbyterian Witness*, *Saint John Daily Telegraph* and the *Wesleyan*.

Selected Websites

"America's First Professional Theatrical Club." History of the Lambs. Accessed May 28, 2011. http://www.the-lambs.org.

Broome, Fiona. "Amherst — The Great Amherst Mystery." March 21, 2008. http://www.hollowhill.com/misc.amherst-mystery/.

"The Cox Family in Sackville, NB." Accessed June 5, 2011. http://www3.telus.net/chignecto/chapman/aqwg09.htm.

"The Great Fire of Saint John, New Brunswick 1877." New Brunswick Museum. Accessed July 2, 2011. http://www.website.nbm-mnb.ca/CAIN/english/sj_fire/.

Hubbell, Walter. *The Haunted House: A True Ghost Story* (1879). Accessed September 7, 2010. http://gaslight.mtroyal.ca/amherst.htm.

Malcolmson, Patricia E. *English Laundresses: A Social History, 1850-1930* (1986). Accessed June 15, 2010. http://washergenes.wordpress.com/2006/06/15/english-laundresses-a-social-history-1850-1930.

Ortega, Javier. "'Pepper's Ghost' Illusion." October, 12, 2009. http://www.ghosttheory.com/2009/10/12/peppers-ghost-illusion.

Pleasants, Helene. "Walter Franklin Prince." *The Biographical Dictionary of Parapsychology* 1964). Accessed April 23, 2011. http://www.pflyceum.org/374.html.

Porrazzo, Jean. "March of Progress: The Rise and Decline of Shoe City, U.S.A." *The Enterprise*. September 24, 2007. http://www.wickedlocal.com/brockton/town_info/history/x1649539547.

"Shannahan Family Marriage Records." Holy Family Parish, Amherst, NS. Accessed May 14, 2010. http://www.holyfamilyparishamherst.org/history-chapter-03.htm.

Temple, L. Parker. "Temple and Related Lines in North America." Updated July 22, 2011. http://www.temple-genealogy.com/index.htm.

Photo Credits

Guy Cox p. 7

B. Thompson p. 9, 11, 73, 89, 90

Collections Canada p. 15

Cumberland County Museum p. 17, 18, 19, 20, 23, 44, 67, 72, 119, 134, 157

North Cumberland Historical Society p. 25

Maritime Conference United Church of Canada p. 27

Public Domain p. 83

Kathy Hufnal p. 94

Penny Lane p. 99

Nova Scotia Archives and Records Management p. 108

Peter Seitl p. 140

Downtown Amherst Revitalization Society p. 155

Index

Page numbers in italics refer to images.

A

Alward, Dr. Aaron 40–41, 100, 105
American Society of Psychical Research 76, 86, 115–16
Amherst Baptist Church 33, 35
Amherst Boot and Shoe Company 16–17, *19–20*, 21, 77, 135, 147
Amherst Cemetery 77, *90*
Amherst Court House 71, *72*
Amherst Gazette 31, 34, 41, 42, 48, 49, 64, 112, 113
Amherst jail *73*, 74
Amherst Methodist Church 27, 53, 55, 66, *67*, 69
Amherst, Nova Scotia *15*, *18*, *119*, *134*, *157*
Amherst Sentinel 74, 114
Atlantic Monthly 124, 125

B

Banner of Light 59, 64, 113
Beck, Captain James 41
Beelzebub. *See* Devil
Bible 14, 33, 66, 68, 107
    Old Testament 107, 124
Bishop, Washington Irving 91–92
Black, J. Albert 28–31, 49, 93, 100, 104, 121
Bliss, James 68, 71, 95
Borley Rectory 151–52
Boston, Massachusetts 43, 45, 52, 59, 64, 82–83
Brockton, Massachusetts 82, *83*, 84, 85–86, 88, *89*, 115, 157
Brockton Times 87–89

C

Calvary Cemetery *88–89*
Canadian Tire 95, 154, 156
Carrick, Mary 126–27, 130
Carrington, Hereward 76, 86–87, 92, 115–116, 121
Carritte, Dr. Thomas
    and diagnoses of Esther 5, 26, 40, 100, 105–7, 112–13, 114–15, 141–42, 149
    and the supernatural 22, 25, 27, 28–30, 36–37, 122, 130
Chatham, New Brunswick 53, 55–58
Chignecto Post
    and Dr. Carrite 106, 107, 112
    and Esther Cox 22– 26, 28, 31, 35, 37, 39, 63, 77
    and Great Amherst Mystery 69, 112–13, 114–15
    and J. Albert Black 28, 49, 104
    reports from 35, 71, 73, 128–29, 131
    and Reverend Temple 110, 112, 130, 138
    and Walter Hubbell 69, 93, 122
Clay, Reverend Dr. Edwin 25, 26, 36, 37, 38–39, 77, 106, *108*, 128
Colchester Sun 38
Cottin, Angélique 124–25
Cox, Abigail 142
Cox, Archibald Thompson 6, 7, 8, 41, 82
Cox, Archibald T. Jr 7

Index

Cox, Esther Logan (Fisher) 6
  Sampler belonging to *140*
Cox, Esther (Shannahan) 89, *155*
Cox, George 13, 144
Cox, Jennie
  background of 13, 14, 91, 144
  and Dunlap and Co. 16, 77
  and Esther's incarceration 74
  and the supernatural 3–4, 6, 25–27, 30–31, 36, 40, 64, 134–35, 145, 154
  and Walter Hubbell 51, 63–64, 66
Cox, Nellie 9, 13, 20, 31, 54, 62, 79, 144, 147
Cox, William 4, 5, 6, 13, 58, 134–35, 144, 149
Cumberland County Court 69–70
Cumberland Railway and Coal Company 79, 81
Cutten, Justice William 71, 77

D

Davidson, Arthur 69–72, 74–75, 138, 141, 146
Davidson, Mary 69, 70, 71
Devil 61, 62, 66, 97
Dickey, Eleazar Boyd 8, 80
Downtown Amherst Revitilization Society Mural 154–*155*
Dunlap and Cook Co. *17*
Dunlap, James 16, 25

E

Eastville, Nova Scotia 6, 9, *10, 11,* 12
Elders. *See also* Presbyterianism 10
Evangelical Advocate 55

F

Fairville, New Brunswick 40, 95
Fisher, Maggie 51, 62, 63, 65, 69, 71, 76, 105, 137
Fisher, Mary 51, 137
Fox, Katie 101–4, 132, 134
Fox, Maggie 101–2, 104, 132, 134
Foyster, Reverend Lionel Algernon 151–52

G

God 61, 66, 107–8, 113, 124
Grandmother Dickey 8–9, 10, 13, 146

H

"Halifax Mystery". *See* "Mr. M"
Halifax, Nova Scotia 8, 35, 39, 43–44, 46, 47, 50, 52, 55, 152
Hubbell, Walter *44*
  and Atlantic Victorian Theatre 43, 47, 52, 69, 77, 117
  as Aguila 92, *94*
  and exhibition of Esther 45–48, 50–52, 56–57
  and spiritualism 64, 91–92, 104
  and the supernatural 51–53, 58, 59–66, 68–69, 75, 100, 105, 110–12, 116–18, 120, 121–123, 130, 135–137, 145
  and "The Haunted House" 69, 76, 93, 115–18, 121–22, 132, 137, 143, 146, 147, 148, 152–53, 157
Hutchinson, Robert 48–50

I

Indian medicine man. *See* Mi'kmaq medicine man

L

Leslie, Bill 154–156
Leslie, Kent 154–155

M

Machias, Maine 8, 41–42, 82
MacNeill, Bob *99*
  background of 17–20, 96–98
  as Bob Nickle ("Bob") 26, 40, 51, 61–63, 66, 69, 71, 75, 76, 136–138, 153
  disappearance of 21, 95, 96, 147, 148, 149
  and Esther Cox 19–21, 98, 100, 112, 117–18, 144, 146–49
  and mesmerism 110–12, 120
MacNeill, Eldon 98
MacNeill, Eliza 51, 136

MacNeill, Robert Nelson 18, 98, 99
MacNeill, Susan 96, 97–98
Malagash, Nova Scotia 14, 17, 40, 96, 97, 136
McIntosh, Ann 8, 41, 82
Mesmer, Franz 109
Mi'kmaq medicine man 76, 112, 122
Moncton Daily Times 46, 52–53, 63
Moncton Dispatch 54
Moncton, New Brunswick 43, 47, 52–53, 56–57, 63, 141
Montreal Gazette 115
Mother Coo 80
"Mr. M" 127–29, 152

N
Nannary, William 43, 47, 52, 77
Nash, Eleanor 81, 82, 84
Nickle, Bob. *See* MacNeill, Bob as Bob Nickle ("Bob")

O
Owen, Robert Dale 124–25

P
Philadelphia, Pennsylvania 45, 64, 95, 151
Pictou County, Nova Scotia 6, 78, 79, 80, 81, 91
Pipes, William T. 71, 74
Porter, Adam 78–81
Porter, James (son of Esther Cox and Adam Porter) 79–80, 82, 84–85, 88
Presbyterianism. *See also* Elders 10, 12, 55
Presbyterian Witness 35, 55, 129
Price, Harry 151, 152
Prince, Dr. Walter Franklin 116–17, 135, 152–53
Princess Street 23

R
Ralph, Louisa Ann (MacNeill) 98, 99
Rogers, William Henry 35–37, *108*
Ruddick's Hall 47, 52–54, 141

S
Sackville, New Brunswick 20, 31, 33, 38, 152, 153
Saint John Daily Telegraph 40, 46, 63, 95–96, 113–14, 127
Saint John, New Brunswick 40, 41, 42, 43, 47, 69, 95, 104, 105, 129
Salem Village Witch Hysteria 123–24, 130
Satan. *See* Devil
Shannahan, Albert 84, 85, 86, 89
Shannahan, John 81, 82, 84
Shannahan, Margaret (daughter of PS) 81, 82, 84
Shannahan, Margaret (mother of PS) 82
Shannahan, Mary 81, 84
Shannahan, Peter 81, 82, 84–85, 86, 88, *89*, 116
Shannahan, Peter Andrew (son of Peter Shannahan and Esther Cox) 84, 85, 88
Shannahan, Sarah 84, 88
Snowden, James 20, 31
Springhill Advertiser 81
Springhill, Nova Scotia 78–82, 84
Springside United Church 9, 10
St. Clair, David 153–54
Stewiacke, Nova Scotia 6, 8–9, 11, 79, 137, 154

T
Teed, Daniel
and Amherst Boot and Shoe Company 16, 77, 137
background of 5, 12, 14
and Esther Cox 5, 14, 21, 31–32, 66, 74, 86, 107, 115, 120, 130, 134–35, 143–44, 146, 148
and family 79, 89–90
home of 13–14, 39, 50, 62, 65, 68, 76, 86, 95, 135, 144, 148
and James Bliss 68, 72
and religion 14, 66, 69, 107, 122
and the supernatural 17, 20, 30, 32–33, 37, 39–40, 65–66, 68, 93, 121, 128, 136

and Walter Hubbell 51, 63, 68,
    93, 117
Teed, Eleanor 18, 65
Teed, George 50, 60, 61, 77, 79, 91,
    149
Teed, John 13, 14, 16, 58, 134–135,
    144
Teed, Mr. 96, 97
Teed, Olive 90
  background of 8, 12, 13–14,
    89–90, 144
  and Esther Cox 31–32, 66, 74, 76,
    86, 107, 116, 143, 146, 147–48,
    149
  and family 14, 16, 77, 79, 89, 149
  home of 13, 16, 76, 86, 95, 144
  and religion 14, 61, 69, 107, 122
  and the supernatural 5, 28, 32, 39,
    40, 60, 66, 93, 104, 115, 130,
    134
  and Walter Hubbell 47, 51, 58, 93,
    115, 121
Teed, Peter 51, 136
Teed, William 16, 77, 91
Temperance Telegram 40
Temple, Reverend Robert Alder 14,
    18, 26, 27, 28, 66, 100, 107, 110,
    112–13, 120, 121, 130, 138
Thompson, Barb 156–57
Trenholm, Constable John 39–40
Tupper, Reverend Dr. Nathan 16,
    26, 109
Tupper, Sir Charles 16, 17

U
United Empire Loyalist 6, 14, 78

V
Van Amburgh, John 42, 68, 71–72,
    141, 146

W
Wesleyan 55, 100–101, 110, 118
White, Frederick 32, 49, 136, 145
White, John
  and Esther Cox 32–33, 36, 38, 43,
    49, 58, 136, 138, 141, 146
  exhibition of 46–48, 52–53,
    56–57
  and the supernatural 32–33, 36,
    49, 51–52, 136
  and Walter Hubbell 46–47, 50–52,
    56–58
  and White's Oyster Saloon 33–34,
    36, 48–49, 58, 136
  and William Rogers 36–37
White, Sarah 32, 33, 50
Williams, Matilda 129, 152
Willis, H. A. 126–27

Y
Yankee Doodle 24, 36, 52

About the Authors

A native of Cumberland County, Laurie Glenn Norris is the author of *Cumberland County Facts and Folklore*. She holds degrees in anthropology and education, and a master's degree in art history. Laurie lives in Lower Kingsclear, New Brunswick, with her husband, Barry Norris, along with lots of books and cats.

Barbara Thompson has been involved in the history museum and heritage field for twelve years. She was the director/curator of the Cumberland County Museum in Amherst and is currently director of DesBrisay Museum in Bridgewater. Trained in commercial design, Thompson spends much of her time researching women's lives and watercolour painting. She currently lives in Bridgewater, Nova Scotia.